GRILLING, SMOKING, and BARBECUING

Also by A. D. Livingston

Cast-Iron Cooking
Good Vittles
Outdoor Life's Complete Fish & Game Cookbook

GRILLING, SMOKING,

and
BARBECUING

A.D.
LIVINGSTON

L&B

Lyons & Burford, Publishers

For Bill

ILLUSTRATIONS BY RICHARD HARRINGTON.

Printed in the United States of America

10 9 8 7 6 5 4 3

Library of Congress Cataloging-in-Publication Data

Livingston, A. D., 1932-
    Grilling, smoking, and barbecuing / A.D. Livingston.
        p. cm.
    Includes index.
    ISBN 1-55821-151-9
    1. Outdoor cookery. 2. Barbecue cookery. I. Title.
TX823.L58 1992   92-4776
641.7′6--dc20   CIP

CONTENTS

Acknowledgments

A few of the recipes and parts of the text for this book were first published in *Sports Afield* magazine and have been reprinted here in slightly modified form. Also, I want to thank my friends for the recipes, advice, and inspiration that have been so freely given on the patio, at the dinner table, in the barber shop, over the telephone, and through the mail.

FOREWORD

In addition to this work, I have written three cookbooks and seven books on other subjects. While some aspects of writing have become easier for me over the years, this particular book has been, apart from the sheer fun of it from a cooking standpoint, much more difficult than the others to organize and conclude. Part of the problem is that there are so many different kinds of grills these days, all of which require adjustments in cooking techniques if predictable results are to be achieved. Even different sizes of the same grill design can make a big difference, and, on the patio, a good deal depends on which way the wind is blowing.

In desperation, I have looked into several other books on the subject and have found that the problem, for the most part, is either ignored or side-stepped. One large-format book with pretty pictures, for example, says that all the recipes were cooked over charcoal in a kettle grill in which the distance of the meat to the heat was fixed at 6 inches. Well, will the recipes work with another shape grill? Or a smaller kettle grill?

The best approach to a book like this, I decided after long suffering and much good eating, is to first cover direct grilling, in which the meat is placed directly over hot coals and is cooked, uncovered, by radiant heat. The minute a hood is closed over the meat, however, the direct heating concept is no longer pure and is complicated by "oven" heat, or convective heat. On the other hand, a hood is often quite handy to have, especially if one wants more smoke flavor in the meat. Nonetheless, there is considerable advantage in learning to cook directly over coals. Once one masters the basic techniques, they can be varied to suit a particular grill or circumstance. Some campgrounds, for example, have fixed grills that have no covers and anyone knowledgeable in direct grilling techniques would have few problems in using such a rig.

Second, the complete patio chef who enjoys cooking large chunks of meat ought to be familiar with the indirect cooking technique. Ideally, this is accomplished with a large covered grill such as the old homemade 55-gallon drum smoker—so ugly that it has to be hidden before the guests arrive. But the technique of indirect cooking can also be adapted for use on a kettle-shaped grill or a modern gas-heated unit with a glass door, sitting spic-and-span beside the sparkling pool.

Is there one grill that will do everything? Yes. Almost. It's the big covered-wagon type grill with a large cooking surface. (Ideally, it should have a meat rack almost three feet long.) These can be used for direct grilling, for indirect cooking, and for smoking. But they are heavy, usually with cast-iron grids, and can't easily be taken along on a canoe trip.

What does the beginner need to start? A grill rack and a sack of charcoal will do fine. Put the charcoal on the ground, box it in with bricks, and put the rack on top. From this simple start, one can go on to easy-to-light gas or electric grills, or work into the joys of cooking over real wood coals. Or stay with charcoal, perhaps with the purchase of a kettle grill or even a large covered wagon grill.

In any case, the objective is to cook good food for yourself and others, and to have fun doing it.

But I'm still not satisfied with the shape of the book and probably never will be. Even the title has caused me much tossing and turning during the night. Part of the problem is in the definition of the terms "grilling," "broiling," "smoking," and "barbecuing." But perhaps I worry too much, and, to be honest, I've been sleeping better ever since I dipped into a book called *Barbecue with Beard*, written by none other than the great James Beard and billed by its publisher as a cooking classic with over 200,000 copies in print. In this work I quickly found a recipe called *Pan-Broiled Chickenburgers*. Good stuff, to be sure, but is it **barbecue**? What about the recipes for *Chicken Cacciatori* or *Veal Scallopini* on pages 148 and 149? *Peaches in Cognac*? What's going on here? Could *Roast Turkey Flambé* be considered barbecue? Maybe, but not in Texas. *French Fried Zucchini*? Never!

—A. D. Livingston
January, 1992

Part One

GRILLSMANSHIP

In this section I discuss such basics as the source of the heat used
for grilling, the importance of grill size, how to deal with flare-ups,
and so on, as well as touching on such questions as whether or not
to sear meat during the cooking process. Accessories and gadgets
are covered, but I try to stop short of post-mounted dinner bells
and chefs' aprons.

FUEL & HEAT

When talking to a Mexican farmer the other day, I asked for his secret of grilling goat. He said that you put the goat on a pole and cook him over hot coals.

"Charcoal?" I asked.

"Something better," he said a little hesitatingly, as if not sure that he should say such words to a gringo.

"Mesquite?"

"¡Sí!" His grin revealed a row of large front teeth, one of gold.

As it turned out, however, he didn't want *smoke* from the mesquite. He wanted only the heat. To accomplish this, he always built a good mesquite fire away from the cooking area. When the wood burned down, he shoveled some of the coals into a fire pit under the goat. Although he used only a modest amount of coals under the goat, he liked to maintain a big fire so as to insure enough hot coals to finish cooking.

In other parts of Mexico, charcoal is made from mesquite, and it is highly prized as a fuel. Some of it is made merely by partly burying wood under the dirt, then building a fire over it. Anyone can make hardwood charcoal in this manner, and I have made it successfully in my home fireplace by partly covering hickory chunks with ashes before building a hot fire, and by first building a wood fire and then partly covering it with ashes.

In my opinion, hardwood charcoal chunks are better than briquets for grilling. Charcoal burns better and hotter and more interestingly. But the pieces are of irregular shape, and each fire made with it is different from the last. My problem is that charcoal has not been readily available in most of the places where I have lived. Charcoal, however, including some from Mexico, can be purchased by mail order.

Whatever I say here, most Americans currently use charcoal briquets and will continue to do so. (I count myself among them.) Briquets are made by pressing powdered charcoal and binder additives into a mold of convenient shape. These briquets burn for a relatively long time, and at a relatively low temperature, making the results more predictable than hot wood coals. (Unprocessed charcoal burns hotter than briquets.) One advantage of briquets is that they are the same convenient size and shape, and are easily distributed in a firebox. Some people even count the exact number of briquets to use for a specific kind of cooking.

At one time, chunks of hard coal were used for grilling. Coal is not a bad choice even today—if you can find it on the market. It burns much hotter than charcoal and lasts for a long time.

But there's no question about it. The ubiquitous briquet, available in every grocery store and every convenience shop in the land, has become America's favorite patio fuel. It is likely to remain so, in spite of the competition from convenient gas and electric grills. Why? For one reason, men (or at least some of us) like to build a fire and consider it to be part of the patio cooking experience. Although I do prefer hardwood or unpressed charcoal, I'll allow that today's briquets are convenient, easy to obtain, and do a pretty good job. That's why I use them more often than not.

Whether you use briquets or charcoal, remember that each burns best if it is bone dry. Store it in a dry place, preferably in an airtight container. A garbage can with a lid will do.

If I use briquets, I usually let the fire burn itself out when I finish cooking. Charcoal, on the other hand, can be reused. Put the fire out with water or cut off the oxygen supply. Even if you use water, the charcoal can be dried out and used again. It is rather porous, so that when dried it's almost as good as new. Briquets tend to disintegrate and crumble after they have been partly burned and then wetted down. I might add that charcoal is rather expensive, and is certainly worth saving.

While speaking of expense, I should say that neither charcoal nor briquets make cheap fuel. I have bought small packages of charcoal at convenience stores that cost more than the meat I was cooking. You'll save some money if you shop around and buy in large bags. As a rule, the more convenient the briquet package, the more it costs. This comment applies to all self-starting briquets that contain lighter fluid (or material), and small packages designed to cook only one meal. But I'll admit that I do sometimes buy a small bag of charcoal that produces a good fire by merely sticking a match to the end of the paper bag. This is neat for tailgating, where you don't want a messy bag of charcoal or lighter fuel to haul around in the van or wagon.

Whenever I've got plenty of time, I really prefer to cook with wood instead of charcoal. But it is more difficult to use, especially when it is freshly cut. Green wood is sometimes used in large barbecue pits, where lots of smoke is wanted. In the past, other fuels, such as corncobs or buffalo chips, have been used for cooking, but usually because of their availability when other fuels are hard to come by.

Of course, the packaged wood chips and chunks for sale at outdoor cooking outlets are intended to produce smoke, not heat. These are usually soaked for some time in water before use. Smoking is discussed at more length in Part Four.

BUILDING A FIRE

Some years ago I joined a Boy Scout troop, but I lost confidence in the outfit on our very first overnight outing. The scout master piddled around with the fire for 30 minutes. He was trying to cut notches into a green pine limb and wouldn't have any of the fat "lightard" knot that I had found for him. This stuff, I knew, would do a quick job because it contains lots of turpentine in it. We called it "lightard," not lightwood. It can be found here and there in the woods in the form of knots about the size of your fist. I assume they are knots from tree limbs or trunks. A similar kindling can be found in longer pieces from stumps and aged timber. The best lightard comes from longleaf pine, which, unfortunately, isn't available all over the country, unless you want to order it by mail. For a long while, I owned a large house that my grandfather had built of heart pine, and over the years it turned to lightwood. You couldn't drive a nail into the walls, and even had a hard time drilling a hole into it. I sold the house, but if I had it back I would think seriously about tearing it down, chopping it up, and selling it in small bundles. Yes, the wood was that "fat," as we said. You could put a wood stove or heater close to the wall and pure turpentine would seep out, ruining the paint job.

There are plenty of fat lightard stumps in the ground in the Southeast, but these are difficult to split and usually don't make straight pieces. Since they never rot, they were, and still are, trouble for farmers in some fields simply because they are so difficult to get out of the ground. In Florida, these old stumps are somehow removed from the ground in large numbers and loaded onto railroad cars and shipped off for commercial use. I've seen a mile or more of loaded cars leaving the vicinity of Perry, Florida, heading north.

In any case, if you are lucky enough to have an old house or a good stump that has been in the ground for about a hundred years, you're in business. Split off a few splinters with a hatchet and use them sparingly to kindle a small fire. Add a few small pieces of ordinary wood, then place larger pieces of wood on top. The same technique can be used with charcoal or briquets. When you are sure of a burn, pile on as many pieces as you think you'll need, keeping them in the shape of a cone or pyramid. After the briquets are covered with a gray ash (or turn from black to gray), you are ready to cook. If you are grilling directly, you'll need coals under the area where the meat or food will be placed, so spread the coals out. For smoking and indirect grilling, it may be best to leave the coals in a pile.

I prefer a charcoal or briquet fire built by the above procedure partly because I enjoy making it work, and because it doesn't require the use of lighter fluids, self-starting briquets, or electrical starters. Frankly, I don't like the smell of the starter fluid. Although I have read that it will not impart a bad flavor to food if it is properly used, I still don't care for it. But I quickly admit that I use fluids and other starting aids from time to time (more often than not, probably). And there are indeed some very convenient fire-starting aids on the market.

One of the best gadgets for the patio chef is a bucket-type briquet starter. Several of these are manufactured, or you can make your own from a large can or a suitable bucket. Remove both ends, so that you have a cylinder. With an old beer can opener, used before pull tabs were invented, make a series of holes along the bottom of the cylinder. Rig a wire bail, or arched handle, and devise a suitable hook. Put the cylinder into your grill firebox. Loosely wad up a sheet of newspaper and stuff it into the cylinder. Pack it down a little. Fill with charcoal. Then light the paper through one of the holes in the bottom. As soon as the coals are burning all the way up, pick up the can, thereby leaving the coals. Smooth out the coals and you're ready to cook. I like these starters for use in small grills partly because they also act as a gauge to the amount of charcoal that you use. Many of us want a fire that is big enough—but not too big. And most of us invariably use more briquets than we really need to do the job.

Electrical fire starters, designed to go under a pile of charcoal, work nicely and are recommended. But don't depend on them entirely. Sometimes I can't find mine—and an electrical outlet isn't always at hand. Or I'll need an adapter to go from 3-prong to 2-prong electric connections. I also use a hair dryer from time to time to help make a hot fire quickly, and, I understand, a battery operated blower is available. Of course, the blower provides lots of oxygen, acting just like the old-fashioned bellows that blacksmiths used.

While watching TV during the war with Iraq, I noticed a street vendor in Baghdad cooking kabobs over a small brazier. He used a hand-held fan to kindle the coals. Remember the trick. It works nicely and doesn't require batteries or electrical outlets. In camp, a palmetto frond, trimmed to size, might save lots of huffing and puffing.

EASY HEAT

Several models and sizes of electrically heated and gas-heated grills are marketed today. All of these, if they are in good working order, are quick to start and easy to use, as compared to wood- or charcoal-burning units. Both gas and electricity are also much cheaper than lump charcoal or briquets. (Wood is also expensive unless you cut your own.) On the other hand, gas and even electrical grills have more parts that can burn out or otherwise fail. They require more preventive maintenance and, in general, require better care.

Usually, both gas and electric grills are rectangular in shape and have hinged hoods. (Roundish kettle grills are, however, made with both gas and electric heating elements, but they are not very common in most parts of the country.) Various kinds of grills and smokers are discussed in the sections on grilling, smoking, and indirect cooking, simply because a good deal depends on how the various kinds of grills are used. Some are ideally suited for indirect cooking or smoking, and others are not. Meanwhile, here are some more general thoughts and guidelines specifically about electric and gas grills.

ELECTRIC GRILLS

These grills are quite handy, if an electrical outlet is near the cooking area. They are usually a little smaller than gas-heated units, and many are designed to sit atop a table. Some smokeless models can even be used in the house; usually, these have some sort of reflector in the bottom that permits the fatty drippings to be drained off without causing smoke or fire. Some other kinds of electric grills are used with lava rocks, which catch and hold the drippings, producing some smoke.

Personally, I like the electric grills with lava rocks for direct grilling of steaks and fish, where relatively thin pieces are cooked. As a rule, the grid is quite close to the fire, which makes the units difficult to use for cooking whole chickens or roasts. However, most of the better units have a heat control knob that permits a wide range of temperatures. When the hood is down, it is possible to cook large pieces of meat, but, still, the units are not very good for indirect cooking. Some of the units can be fitted with an electric rotisserie, and these are highly recommended for those chefs who want to cook large chunks of meat over these small electric units.

Before buying an electric grill, make sure that you can purchase replacement heating coils from the retailer or from the manufacturer. These burn out from time to time, especially when they are covered or partly covered with grease-soaked lava rocks.

Electric grills are convenient and do a good job on the porch or patio.

COOKING WITH GAS

A number of gas-heated grills are on the market, most of which are used with lava rocks, ceramic nuggets, or some sort of "radiant" grating. The tiny grills that use little bottles of gas are designed for people on the move, such as campers or tailgaters. Most of the patio-model gas grills use larger portable tanks of LP gas. Some models even tap into a natural gas line. All of these units can be used for direct grilling, and they are quite easy to use. They can be ignited by a pushbutton self-starter, or they can be lit with a match. Most of the gas grills have adjustable heat, which is a great feature.

Some of the better and larger units have heating elements on either side, both of which have independent heat control valves. The two-burner kinds are almost necessary for indirect cooking. But, even so, these units are not ideal for indirect cooking simply because they are not large enough for true

Grills heated by bottled gas are quick to start and easy to use.

indirect heat. In other words, there simply isn't enough distance between the heat source and a large chunk of meat. For one thing, the heating elements go all the way to the middle of the grill, whereas the charcoal fire in a regular grill can be pushed all the way to the end. But this is a relative matter, and indirect cooking can surely be accomplished on a gas grill, although the chef might have to turn the meat from time to time, exposing all the sides to the direct heat. On the other hand, the complete grillsman might argue that there are advantages in having one end of a roast or ham closer to the heat source. This matter is discussed further under the "Grill Size" heading below.

In the past, most of the gas grills have come with lava rocks to form a layer on a gridwork above the heat. When new, these rocks work just right, and, personally, I like the way they soak up the fatty drippings. In time, however, the rocks tend to disintegrate and have to be replaced. These days, instead of lava rocks, more and more people are using a harder, less porous substance that is molded into uniform pieces, and this trend toward various kinds of ceramic and other manmade nuggets will likely continue. My guess is that in time individual rocks or pieces will not be widely used. Instead, we will have radiant plates of various sorts that can be inserted over the gas heating element.

Obviously, gas grills in good working order are much easier to use than those that use charcoal. Some purists, however, maintain that charcoal produces a better flavor in the finished product. Others claim that neither burning charcoal nor gas-heated rocks have flavor, and that the smoke is from burnt grease or from wood chips. I tend to agree that neither gas nor charcoal flavors the meat one way or the other. (But I am suspicious of the self-starting charcoal and of lighter fluids.) Genuine wood coals, in my opinion, are a different matter and do impart a pleasant flavor to the meat as well as smelling better during the cooking process. But that's just one man's opinion.

Although the gas grills can be quite easy to use, they can also be a pain in the neck. Here are some things to consider before buying one:

RUNNING OUT OF GAS. After this work was almost finished, my editor reminded me that the portable tanks used with gas grills have a way of running out just when the steak is half done. He made a very good point, and he says that I ought to recommend that anyone who owns a gas grill with portable tanks should purchase two tanks. I agree with what he says, but I add that it's just a matter of time before most of us would have two empty tanks on hand! In any case, remember to have your tank refilled before you need it. Although some of these are equipped with gauges, these are not often accurate.

SAFETY. Gas is surely more dangerous than charcoal. Check for leaks. Follow the manufacturer's instructions for storage. In use, closing the hood too quickly has been known to put out the fire, at least on some models, and this can be quite hazardous.

HOT SPOTS. Not all gas grills burn properly, due to clogged or partly clogged holes in burner element. Uneven heat can, of course, cause meat to be cooked improperly. A friend of mine tells me that he even saw one grill that would burn a hole in thin steaks. Sometimes cleaning the heating element, making sure that none of the port holes in the burner are clogged up, will solve this problem. If not, check for cracks in the heating element.
Also, improper distribution of lava rocks can cause uneven heating.

MAINTENANCE AND STORAGE. As stated elsewhere, gas grills require proper maintenance and storage if they are to work properly over a long period of time. The burner elements can cause problems, and should be cleaned according to the manufacturer's instructions. Any clogged burner portholes should be cleaned out with a piece of wire. The push-button starters may also require cleaning from time to time. Pressure regulating valves and other fittings must be kept in proper working order. Proper storage of both the grill and the gas tank will help keep things working. It is best to follow the manufacturer's instructions to the letter.

CLEANING. Apart from regular maintenance, modern gas grills seem to require more cleaning than regular grills. Most of them are attractive when new, and even have glass windows in the hood. The windows are almost impossible to keep clean and, in my opinion, are not very practical. Special cleaning compounds are available for the windows as well as for other parts of the grill. Some people even clean the inside of the grill, as if it were an oven in the house.

NONADJUSTABLE GRIDS AND GRATES. I like to have the option of changing the distance from the meat to the fire either by raising the meat rack or by lowering the fire grate. Thus, I use one setting for grilling a steak quickly and quite another for slowly cooking chicken quarters. On the other hand, the heat on most gas grills can be turned up or down, thereby making up at least partly for nonadjustable grates.

One advantage to gas grills is that the same tank, with the aid of a Y fitting, can be used to fuel fish fryers, burners for skillets or pots, and so on. In fact, at least one gas grill is marketed with an auxiliary burner fixed on one side of the grill, and kits are available for attaching auxiliary burners where the end shelf is usually installed.

GRILL SIZE

A large grill is almost always better than a small one for indirect grilling. The reason is that you need some distance between the meat and the fire, lest one end of the meat get too hot from direct heat and cook quicker than the other end. (On the other hand, the complete grillsman might argue that having the larger part of a ham or other piece of meat closer to the heat can be an advantage.) For indirect cooking with rectangular grills, I recommend a large covered grill with the grate at least 30 inches from one end to the other. The depth or width of the grill isn't quite as important, since it is the length that usually separates the meat from the fire in indirect cooking.

I must add that at the time of this writing it is hard to find such a grill in most outlets simply because the smaller units are cheaper and therefore sell better to the masses. If you find a large grill on display at some store, it's easy enough to measure or guess at the length. When ordering from catalogs, however, you may have to write or call for more information, or do some guesswork. Note that the length given in the catalog will often include wooden shelves on either end. Note also that the square inches of cooking area can also be misleading. I've seen gas grills advertised as having almost 680 square inches of cooking area. When I first saw this figure, I perked up considerably because such a grid would be larger than my favorite charcoal grill, the CB940, which has 665 square inches of cooking area (figured from a grid length of 35 inches and width of 19 inches). But the catalog said "dual level" cooking area. I first thought that maybe this meant that the grid could be adjusted to several levels, which was too good to be true. Before ordering, however, I figured out that the "dual level" meant that an auxiliary rack came with the unit, which sat atop the main rack. Yet, this auxiliary rack wasn't shown in the photograph of the unit. What was shown was a rib rack for vertical cooking. The length specified for the unit included the shelves, so that, in short, it was difficult to tell how large the main cooking rack really was. My guess is that the primary cooking area was about 350 square inches.

The size of the kettle grill is also quite important for indirect cooking, in which the coals are arranged like a doughnut around a drip pan. The larger the unit, the better this works, within reason. These grills are discussed in more detail in Part Three, Indirect Cooking.

HOW HOT IS IT?

As a rule, it takes 30 minutes for a charcoal or a briquet fire to get ready for cooking. This is often pushed somewhat by impatient chefs, but it's better to err on the long side, I think, especially when grilling a couple of steaks that will be done long before the fire expires. Wood fires may take longer to make good coals, depending on the size of the pieces of wood or logs. Gas and electric grills vary, but, still, 30 minutes or less is not a bad figure if you are using lava rocks or some such radiant heating aid.

Most charcoal purists will wait until the briquets or chunks turn gray before they start cooking, especially if the briquets have been squirted with starter fluid.

Once the fire gets a good start, the temperature at cooking level can be varied by increasing or decreasing the distance between the meat and the fire. The intensity of wood and charcoal fires can be adjusted by adding more fuel, by spreading the coals thinner, by opening up or closing down the air intake vent, by fanning the fire, by brushing the ash off the coals, or, sometimes, by squirting water onto the fire to cool it down.

Electric and gas fires can be controlled by adjusting the fuel valves or the rheostat knob. Remember, however, that such adjustments do not result in drastic or fast reduction in the heat of the lava rocks.

A good many recipes call for cooking over a "hot fire" or a "medium fire." These terms are somewhat misleading, or can be, because what's important is the temperature at cooking level. This is usually estimated by counting slowly by one-thousands while the palm of the hand is held directly over the fire, at cooking level, until you have to move it. Each count should equal one second. A count of "one thousand, two thousand, three thousand" indicates a hot fire. A count going up to six thousand indicates a medium fire. A slow fire is mostly a guess. For indirect cooking under a hood, a thermometer is by far the best bet. Most of the thermometers that are built into the hood of a grill are not very accurate, and some are not placed properly for indirect grilling. The best bet is to use a good oven thermometer, placed on the rack near the meat.

FLARE-UPS

Unless wood chips are used, the smoked flavor of meat grilled over charcoal, gas, or electric grills comes from burnt grease or other drippings from the meat. Too much of this smoke may not be agreeable, and too much grease on the coals or heating elements can in fact cause a fire of some magnitude. Such flare-ups can ruin the flavor of good meat, and can set the meat itself ablaze or else char it.

A number of steps can be taken to prevent or control flare-ups. First, it's best as a rule to use meat that doesn't contain much fat. Although the marbled fat in steaks can't be eliminated, and may be desirable from a culinary viewpoint, most of the fat around the edges of a piece of meat can be trimmed off. Chickens, for example, very often carry gobs of fat around the tail section, and this can easily be trimmed away. Cheap hamburger meat often contains much fat and shrinks up considerably on the grill. A more expensive ground meat will (or should) reduce the flare-up problem while yielding a full-sized burger.

Second, a basting sauce that contains lots of butter or oil should be used sparingly, lest it run into the coals.

Third, meat that is grilled close to a hot fire should be watched closely. In case of flare-ups, it's best to move the meat over with tongs to get it off the fire. Obviously, a large grid surface is highly desirable for this kind of cooking.

Fourth, using a hood, when available, will help prevent flare-ups simply by restricting the amount of oxygen. However, using a hood tends to bake the steaks as well as grill them, and may be frowned upon by some experts. (By the same token, some chefs who broil steaks in an oven insist that the door remain open during the cooking process.)

Fifth, cooking the meat farther from the heat source will usually result in fewer and less serious flare-ups. On the other hand, grilling steaks too far from the heat will result in a steak that is cooked through and through instead of being crisply browned on the outside and medium rare in the center.

Sixth, adjusting the heat can help. Some charcoal units have adjustable vents, and, of course, the gas and electric units have knobs for adjusting the heat. But remember that such adjustments do not make for quick results with gas or electric heat if lava rocks or other such radiant aids are used.

Seventh, some people use water to dampen the flame and lower the intensity of the heat. Water for this purpose can be put into some sort of squirt bottle and kept handy, and even water hoses with spray nozzles are used for large cookouts. Of course, water should not be used with electric grills and is not recommended for use with gas grills.

Eighth, move the meat rack away from the heat, if possible. I often grill steaks over hot wood coals with a Big Foot grill, which can be raised or lowered instantly and can also be swung away from the fire. Not everybody will have such a unit, but remember that a grid (or a grilling basket) with a handle can be used either on top of the regular grid or over an open fire. I often grill meat in my home fireplace on the top half of a grilling basket, supported with ordinary building bricks suitably arranged.

Ninth, consider using a drip pan with large pieces of meat that are to be cooked directly over the fire.

Tenth, some gas grills have holes in the bottom to drain out any fat that isn't burned in the lava rock section. If these holes clog up, grease can accumulate in the bottom and cause a fire of some magnitude. Water from a squirt bottle won't extinguish a bad grease fire, but sprinkling baking soda on the area will quickly kill it.

IS IT DONE?

I've always been impressed by seemingly cocksure outdoor chefs who can poke on a piece of meat and pronounce it done. While cooking, rare meat is soft and has no juices standing on the surface; well done meat is firm and tends to have juices on the surface; medium and medium rare are somewhere in between. It is difficult for me to give advice on these matters simply because experience is the best guide and because I rely instead on a good meat thermometer and a clock or timer. Some chefs can tell when a bird is done by twisting or manipulating a leg, testing how easily it moves in the joint. This method has merit, but, again, a meat thermometer works better.

As a rule, however, a thermometer doesn't work too well on steaks or chops less than 2 inches thick. There are several "steak buttons" and an electronic temperature probe that will indicate doneness on some sort of scale. But it's easy enough for the experienced chef to grill a steak without such gadgets. After a while, one simply knows how long it takes to cook a steak, based on heat intensity and the distance from the meat to the heat and the thickness of the meat. If one cooks steaks pretty much the same way all the time, then a timer becomes a reliable guide. In any case, most grillers usually test a representative piece of steak (either a spare or one's own piece) by cutting into it under good light before serving the guests. That's the only foolproof test.

Chicken quarters are especially difficult to grill, and too often they are well done on the outside and far too bloody around the bone. In my opinion, to err on the well done side is better than to serve it too rare. The exception is skinned breast fillets, or fingers, which tend to become too dry. Whole chickens are best when they are grilled on a rotisserie or cooked for a long time by a low-heat indirect method. A whole turkey or turkey breast should always be cooked with the aid of a meat thermometer or a heat button.

Beef and pork roasts, as well as other large cuts such as a leg of lamb, should also be cooked with the a good meat thermometer inserted well into the thickest part of the meat, but not touching the bone. There is no universal agreement on the exact temperature for different kinds of meat, but the following is what I recommend: roast beef, 135 degrees; venison, 135 degrees; lamb, 140 degrees; fresh pork ham, 160 degrees; and turkey or chicken, 170 degrees. Be warned that to be eaten safely, fresh pork and bear should be cooked well done. More and more, rare chicken is also becoming suspect. But it's difficult to be sure of where exactly we stand on these matters. For a long time the U. S. Department of Agriculture recommended that fresh pork be cooked to 185 degrees, but this figure has recently been lowered to 160 degrees, to the delight of all pork-loving epicures.

TO SEAR OR NOT TO SEAR

Some expert chefs argue that meat should first be seared very close to a hot heat source before being cooked longer at a more moderate temperature. The idea is to seal in the juices. Frankly, I have mixed feelings about this matter. While I allow that searing does sometimes help hold in the juices, I believe that it can also make the outside of the meat tough.

Right or wrong, I seldom sear meat that is grilled directly over the coals. My steaks are usually cooked very close to the heat, so that the searing is simply part of the cooking. Those chefs who cook steaks slower might indeed profit by searing the meat if the grill has adjustable racks or if the heat can be quickly controlled.

It is easy to sear large pieces of meat when they are to be cooked by the indirect method in which the fire is on only one side of the grill. First cook the meat directly over the fire to sear it, then move it over for slow cooking or smoking.

I might add that meat is frequently seared or "browned" when it is cooked in the kitchen. Many recipes for roasts and stew meat call for first browning the meat and then cooking it for a long time. I sometimes cook meat without first browning it, as in an Irish stew, and find that the results are good. Also, some chefs sear a steak in a skillet before cooking such good dishes as *steak au poivre*. My choice is to sear the meat on high heat and cook it at the same time. But that's just one man's opinion.

ACCESSORIES & GADGETS

By far the most valuable accessories for the grillsman, or any other chef, who is interested in cooking large chunks of meat is a good meat thermometer, as discussed under the "Is It Done?" section above. Some other accessories are covered in other parts of the book, as applicable to a particular topic. The list below includes some of the more popular accessories and gadgets, along with such indispensable items as a good set of tongs.

ROTISSERIES. Spit-turning electric units are available for many of the covered-wagon grills. Some of these work on household electricity, but battery-powered units are also available. And some work either way. Accessories for the rotisserie include a spit balance for better weight distribution, various fish baskets, tumble baskets, many-pronged spits for hotdogs, and even kabob wheels. There is one large 6-foot grill (the Country Club Grill) that has a rotisserie spit large enough to cook a whole pig along with a 25–pound chunk of meat.

Although the rotisserie is a great idea, especially for long, even cooking of large chunks of meat, not many people take advantage of it. Almost every patio chef buys a rotisserie at one time or another, but few of us actually use it on a regular basis. The electric motor, or possibly its reduction system, is a big problem simply because turning a large piece of meat for a long time is quite a job—especially if the meat is out of balance. Further, the balance seems to shift after a few turns over the fire. One text recommends that out-of-balance meat should be respitted—but one wonders how many spit holes and prong holes should be punched through a good piece of meat.

In any case, spitting the meat properly is more trouble than cooking it by the indirect method. A chicken, for example, must be spitted, secured on either side with prongs, and lashed down at the legs and at the wings. But once the meat is secured and balanced properly on the spit, cooking on a rotisserie is very easy if an internal meat thermometer is used.

TONGS. Whether you are cooking in the kitchen, on the patio, or in camp, good tongs are surely one of the better accessories for turning steaks, chicken quarters, and other pieces of meat on the grill or in the skillet. They can also be used, as I can attest, to tend a charcoal fire, and are handy for turning or moving a single briquet to precisely where it is needed. Although some people use heavy gloves or some other tool to tend their fire, I don't normally have these at hand.

I think that relatively short tongs—only 7 or 8 inches long from one end to the other—work better than long ones. The longer the tongs, the harder they are to use; the shorter the tongs, the better the grip. Since most of the kitchen tongs are 12 or 13 inches long, and most of the patio tongs are 18 or 19 inches long, one may have to shop around for short ones.

In defense of long tongs and other long-handled tools packaged and sold to outdoor chefs, I'll have to say that they are sometimes useful at an open campfire where shifting winds cause a smoke problem. The manufacturers of such gadgets say that they help the chef keep well away from the intense heat. What intense heat? A layer of glowing charcoal in the firebox of a grill can be worked quite close. If one can hold the palm of one's hand at cooking level while counting "one thousand," "two thousand," "three thousand," and so on, then short tongs can certainly be used to turn a steak!

SPATULAS. As stated above, I usually prefer to turn meat with tongs, if possible, instead of sticking forks into it. Spatulas can also be used to turn meat or help turn it, and of course they work better than tongs with hamburgers and thin fish fillets.

FORKS. All sets of barbecue tools will contain at least one long-handled fork. Personally, I have little use for these, except for roasting wieners or marshmallows in my kitchen fireplace or over a campfire. Tongs work better for turning steaks and don't punch holes in the meat, which let the good juices out. Anyone who cooks large pieces of meat, and turkeys, by the indirect method on large covered wagon grills might look around for an old 3–tine pitch fork. Cut the handle off to about 2 feet, and use the business end to lift meat off the grid and onto a platter or pan. The idea is to run the tines under the meat, making use of the slots in the grill, and lift it up, helping things along with tongs or a gloved hand.

BASTING BRUSHES AND MOPS. Any good bristle brush will do for basting, and I have even used paint brushes. I like a round one. Some people use small mops, especially for basting barbecued ribs, but the process gets pretty sloppy, in my opinion. As with forks and tongs, long brushes are not needed and frequently don't work as nicely as short ones.

GRIDS AND RACKS. A wide range of grid shapes and weights are available. I like the heavy-duty cast-iron grids that are standard on some of the larger covered wagon type grills, and these can be purchased in several sizes. These are quite heavy, so be sure to get a grid-lifter tool to help handle them. Some of the lighter wire grills do a good job, but others tend to come apart after repeated use. Also, more and more grills are marketed with porcelain-plated wire grids. These are fine.

There are also some neat fine-mesh auxiliary grids, usually used atop an ordinary grill, that are coated with porcelain. Some of these have a backstop that makes them much easier to turn shrimp, vegetables, and small foods with a spatula. Also, a porcelain-plated "grill wok" is available for stir-grilling vegetables.

Several vertical racks are made for holding slabs of ribs, chickens, ducks, and other good meats in a vertical position. These are especially suitable for use during indirect cooking. The idea, of course, is to save grill space so that enough spare ribs can be cooked to feed everybody.

GRILLING BASKETS. A hinged grilling basket with a long handle is ideal for cooking fish, hamburger steaks, and other meats that are likely to flake and fall apart if they are handled with spatulas or tongs. The idea, of course, is to put the meat inside and flip the whole basket. Normally, the baskets are used atop the grill's regular racks, but they can also be used directly over fires that are build between bricks, logs, or some other suitable props. The long handle makes them ideal for use over a hot campfire, in which case the whole basket or either half can be used. If things go wrong, the whole works can be withdrawn immediately.

I prefer a rectangular basket with an adjustable depth. For most purposes, a 12 × 9 × 2–inch adjustable basket will be fine, in which case the

2-inch depth can be adjusted down to ½ inch or so for thin fish fillets. These rectangular baskets are sometimes called steak baskets, but they are, I think, more often used for hamburgers and pieces of fish. To be sure, a number of other fish baskets are made, some for holding single fish, others for holding two fish, and some for holding three fish. These have cavities shaped like a fish. Still other baskets are made for grilling meat and vegetable kabobs without having to use a skewer. Before buying any of these baskets, except perhaps for an adjustable rectangular basket, remember that they don't work too well with a hood, which, in my opinion, limits their use for indirect cooking.

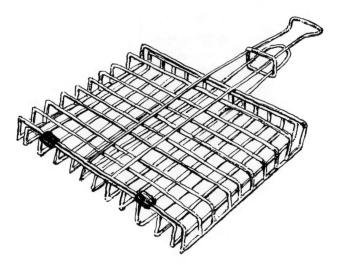

Grilling baskets are recommended for holding burgers, fish, and other hard-to-turn foods.

THERMOMETERS. Some grills with a cover come with a thermometer, and these are highly desirable although most of them are not very accurate. Kits are also available for installing a thermometer on other grills. I prefer that a thermometer be graduated in degrees F., but some read from low to high. Also, an ordinary oven thermometer can usually be placed inside a grill for use in indirect cooking.

GLOVES AND TOWELS. Many people use heavy gloves, even made of asbestos, for adjusting the hot knobs on gas grills, for moving hot charcoal or briquets around, and even for turning and rearranging ribs and other pieces of meat. I seldom use gloves, but I do, however, want a thick kitchen towel around my neck when I am cooking. With it I can adjust a hot knob, pick up a cast-iron sauce pot, or wipe the charcoal smudge off my tongs before turning the steaks. Cooking gloves are good things to have, however, and I plan to hold mine out the next time I run across them for future use. Heavy gloves are especially useful when cooking with cast-iron skillets.

Heavy duty gloves come in handy for tending a hot charcoal fire and for moving large chunks of meat.

GRILL COVERS. Form-fitted plastic or vinyl covers are available for most of the better grills. These are highly desirable for those units that must be stored outside, but they are not necessary for grills that can be stored in a dry shed or other such place. In fact, they may do more harm than good in some storage conditions. Cast-iron grids, I think, do better when they are stored uncovered, ventilated, and dry. In any case, covers are not always necessary. I know one fellow who has cooked almost every weekend on a large covered-wagon grill for over 20 years. He has never used a cover over the grill, but he does store it in a dry place—with the hood open.

28

CLEANING UP

Most of the manufacturers' manuals that come with grills recommend that you clean them up immediately after use. Some books on the subject also recommend the same practice. And the advice seems especially urgent with electrically heated grills, partly because the elements are so quick to burn out. (The water/smoker silo rigs can also be damaged by condensation.) Gas grills, as discussed earlier, must also be cleaned on a regular basis in order to keep the burner elements in good working order.

Some books even recommend that the meat racks in charcoal burners be washed with soap and water. Can you imagine that? I've never known a patio chef who washed his grill with anything. Usually, a wire brush is used—and sparingly—on cast-iron or wire grids. The manufacturers of some porcelain-coated grids warn against cleaning them with a wire brush.

I suppose that it would be best to clean and grease the grid after use, but I would be wasting time to set forth such instruction here. After grilling, smoking, or barbecuing a good piece of meat, most of us are going to say, "To hell with it. Let's eat."

Part Two

GRILLING

The terms "grilling" and "broiling" are used rather loosely in the cookbook and magazine trade, as well as in the restaurant and fastfood business. In this little book, I use the "grilling" to mean cooking meat or other food *over* glowing coals or other heat; "broiling," I say, means cooking meat *under* the source of heat, and is therefore seldom used herein. Other terms, such as "char-broiling" and "pan-broiling" may serve the purposes of some writers and advertising sharps, but I have no use for them. What I'm talking about in this section of this book is grilling directly over hot coals or other source of heat, such as gas heated lava rocks or electrical elements.

EQUIPMENT FOR OPEN GRILLING

All you need for grilling succulent meat is a grid placed directly over a suitable bed of hot coals. Open grills range in size from large units designed to cover a pit barbecue down to a simple rack placed on rocks over a campfire. All of the grills with a firebox can be used for cooking by direct heat, and some have hoods that make them much more versatile and much easier to use. The headings below cover the various types, along with some related topics, such as equipment for use in a fireplace and major accessories for the open grill, such as the rotisserie.

BRAZIERS. This term usually refers to inexpensive grilling units made with a wire rack over a fixed firebox. Normally, they are made of thin metal, with or without legs, and are suitable only for direct grilling. (A disposable unit is made with aluminum, loaded with charcoal briquets.) Usually, these inexpensive units have the grid or grill rack in a fixed position in relation to the coals, and have no venting mechanism to help control the heat. Still, they can turn out some good eating.

HIBACHIS. A favorite everywhere, this style of grill is relatively small but is made from heavy cast iron. (In quality, of course, some are better than others.) They are suitable only for direct grilling, but the better ones have adjustable air vents to help control the heat and a fuel rack that lets ashes fall to the bottom. Some even have adjustable racks, so that you can vary the distance from the heat to the meat. I highly recommend these units for the patio, for the fireplace, and for the tailgate. They are a little heavy for camp use. Remember also that they don't have much cooking surface. But they are perfect for grilling two, maybe three, large T-bones.

Hibachis, often made of heavy-duty cast iron, are excellent for grilling a T-bone or two.

The inexpensive kettle grills, made of heavy sheet metal, are popular models for the home patio.

KETTLE GRILLS. As a rule, these units are larger than the hibachis and are made of rather light metal. All models have a cover, and some have wheels. Many models do not have adjustable racks, so that you must cook at a fixed distance from the coals. Some kettles have adjustable vents, and some don't. All of the kettle grills have a rounded base and hood, and, of course, circular racks.

The larger kettle grills are also used for smoking simply by adding chips or chunks to the hot coals and keeping the hood closed. These units can also be fitted with a drip pan to catch hot grease. This is accomplished by putting a tin biscuit pan (or some such container) in the center of the fire box, then distributing the hot coals around it. The fatty meat, of course, is centered over the drip pan. It's a neat idea, and I've seen it set forth in several books, but I've never known a patio chef who actually used the technique on a regular basis. In any case, the kettle is a highly popular grill, and they are usually not expensive.

COVERED-WAGON AND BARREL GRILLS. The favorite of many serious patio chefs is the large, long grill with a hinged cover. In fact, merely having a hinge on the lid is a big advantage over the kettle grills, especially for those practitioners who like to baste frequently. These grills come in various sizes, and they are also popular designs for gas- and electrically heated units. The large charcoal units, however, with emphasis on size, are the most versatile grills on the market. Most of the large commercial units are made from very sturdy material, and have cast-iron grids. Many of the homemade units are barrel shaped, and in fact are often made by cutting 55–gallon drums in half. I've seen much larger units that were made from storage tanks.

These larger units will be discussed in more detail in the sections on smoking and indirect cooking. For direct grilling, the large units work just fine for large or small orders. If you want to grill a couple of steaks, merely build a small fire and contain it with a couple of brick partitions. On most of these units, you'll have the option of lowering the grid (or raising the fire). You'll also have adjustable vents to help adjust the fire. Further, you'll have plenty of room to move the food around in case of flare-ups, or merely to keep meat hot while more is being cooked. For large orders, some of these units have grids that are almost a yard long and 20 inches wide. By standing between two of these, a friend of mine grills 2,000 chicken wings for his annual managers' meeting.

PARK GRILLS. These grills, usually fixed atop a knee-high structure, are commonly seen in state or federal parks and local recreation areas. (The fire boxes of some of these are placed below ground, and a grid is on top. This design is used in some parks where wind is often a problem.) A few people do have them in their back yards, and at least one model is available commercially. Most of these do a good job with direct grilling, although some of them do not have adjustable grids. Understandably, many of the grids cannot be removed; with these, cleanup can be a problem, but most people who use these units frequently become immune to the grime on the grill, knowing that a hot fire will kill off any bacteria that might be present. Before using the grill, scrape it with a spoon or some such object that fits partway between the grids. If you're really fussy about this, take a wire brush with you.

CAMPFIRE GRILLS. There are a number of grills and grids suitable for cooking over coals at a campsite. Some of these fold up, making a convenient unit for backpackers and others who travel light. My choice is the top part of a grilling basket. Why? Because of the handle. With it I can pick the whole works up off the fire instead of having to move the meat around.

I have recently fallen in love with the Big Foot campfire grill, which, with fingertip control, swings away from the fire. This makes it convenient to turn meat, and or to move the meat from above the fire in case of flare-ups. The Big Foot also has 9 height adjustments, which makes it very easy to get your meat closer to the heat or farther from it. It's a heavy-duty rig, so that the grill will also hold cast-iron Dutch ovens, frying pans, coffee pots, and so on. Further, the grill part is detachable and the handle of the thing can be used to hold pots with bails, coffee pots, and so on. In other words, it's better than a dingle stick, which is what many old camp cooks call a pole that is suspended over the fire. Although the Big Foot was designed for camp cooking, I often use it in my backyard for grilling steaks over a wood fire.

FIREPLACE GRILLS. Several units are available for use in a fireplace, and they range from simple to elaborate. For a small grill, my choice is the top rack of a rectangular grilling basket (or the whole basket) with the handle.

As noted above, this unit can easily be moved on and off the heat. Instead of andirons, I normally put the rack on 3 bricks, or 6 bricks, depending on how high I want the grill from the heat. Remember that I can stack the bricks, and that I can turn either the top or the bottom brick, or both, on its side. This set-up is quite versatile, and, sometimes, I rig two such units in the fireplace. I've also put larger cast-iron grids in the fireplace, atop bricks, to good advantage. If you have a large fireplace in your kitchen, you might take a look at some of the more elaborate units, including a spit. Remember also that some small grills will fit inside the fireplace, and I often cook on a hibachi, especially when the patio is cold, wet, or infested with mosquitoes.

PATIO FIREBOXES. I've seen a neat patio fireplace, portable, that can be fitted with a grill. It is circular (about 30 inches across) and sits on legs. It's really neat for roasting wieners or marshmallows, or for grilling steaks on a chilly evening.

For outdoor cooking over an open wood fire, it's hard to beat the Big Foot grill, which is adjustable and which also swings away from the heat.

GRILLING BEEF

In many ways, beef is a very good meat for grilling. Most of the better cuts, such as T-bone and ribeye steaks, have fat marbled in the tissue, and don't dry out as badly as some other meats. Moreover, beef doesn't have to be cooked well-done, and the meat is widely accepted in America when it is at least pinkish on the inside. For flavor and texture, it's hard to beat a beefsteak that has been properly grilled. Here are some recipes.

Good Ol' Boy Steak

I know dozens of good ol' boys who like to cook steaks on the grill while the little woman makes the salad and bakes the potatoes in the kitchen. Most of these fellows use a covered grill and a rather quick marinade. In my neck of the woods, a large percentage of them use Dale's steak seasoning which can be found in the supermarket. This is a thin liquid, not a thick sauce, and is used for a quick marinade and for basting. It has various ingredients in it, but I suspect that it is mainly soy sauce. It is a concentrated liquid, so not that much of it is needed.

>**steaks**
>**Dale's steak seasoning**
>**seasoning salt** (see note below)
>**pepper** (optional)
>**beer** (for drinking while you cook)

Trim the fat off the steaks, put them onto a non-metallic container (a plate or platter will do), and sprinkle them lightly with the Dale's steak seasoning. Let the steaks marinate for half an hour, while you build the fire and have a beer or two. Adjust the grill so that the steaks will be between 4 to 6 inches from the coals. Sprinkle each steak on both sides with pepper and seasoning salt and put it onto the grill. Close the cover. Cook the steaks for 6 or 7 minutes on each side. While cooking, open the hood once or twice and baste the steaks with more marinade. After basting, sprinkle lightly with seasoning salt. Do not overcook. Before serving, cut into a steak to check it. Cook to order, but medium rare is best. Put the cooked steaks onto a platter and take them into the house. Eat at the table with baked potatoes and tossed salad.

Note: Many of my good ol' boy buddies prefer lemon-pepper seasoning salt. Others use garlic salt, celery salt, or some other mix. Every good ol' boy will have his favorite. Many people will also want to souse the cooked meat with some sort of thick steak sauce. This, to me, is a culinary sin, but I've finally given in on the matter and allow the practice even in my own home, for those who bring their own sauce.

Pepper Steak

One of my favorite meats is a well-peppered T-bone steak cooked in a broiler. The same recipe can be used to advantage for cooking a good steak atop a hot grill. Here's all you'll need:

> **T-bone or ribeye steaks**
> **freshly ground black pepper (see instructions)**
> **salt**

Grind or crush some peppercorns. (The coarse ground black pepper that is packaged in bottles also works pretty well, although its aroma isn't as good as freshly crushed pepper.) Rub the pepper into the steak on both sides. How much pepper you use is a matter of personal taste. I like lots of it because the flavor goes well with good beefsteak. Do not salt the meat at this time. Put the steaks aside for about 30 minutes, or until you build a nice hot fire in the grill.

When the coals are ready, adjust the rack to within 3 or 4 inches of the coals. Put the steaks on the grid and grill each side for 5 or 6 minutes, depending on the thickness of the steaks, how far the grid is from the coals, and so on. Do not overcook. Medium rare is my choice. If in doubt, cut into a steak before serving the batch. It should be pink on the inside. Since it is cooked quite close to hot coals, it should be nicely browned on the outside. Salt each steak lightly a few minutes before serving.

T-bone Rosemary

Here's a recipe that can be used with any good steak, but I usually use it with T-bones or Porterhouses about 1-inch thick. The measures listed below will provide marinade and basting sauce for four T-bones.

> **4 T-bone steaks, trimmed**
> **salt and pepper**
> **1 cup olive oil**
> **¼ cup fresh parsley, minced**
> **2 teaspoons fresh rosemary, minced**
> **3 cloves garlic, minced**

Mix a marinade sauce with the olive oil, freshly ground black pepper, parsley, rosemary, and garlic. (If you use dried parsley and dried rosemary, cut the measures in half.) Place the steaks in a suitable glass container and pour the marinade over them. Turn the steaks to make sure that all sides are coated. Marinate for at least 1 hour.

Build a hot fire in your grill. Remove the steaks from the marinade and drain them slightly. Place the steaks on the grill and cook one side for 4 or 5 minutes. Turn the steak, brush some of the marinade on the browned side, and cook the other side for about 4 minutes, or until the steak is done to your liking. (Medium rare is best.) Before serving the steak, sprinkle both sides very lightly with salt.

A New York Strip Steak, Soused, for Dick Mace

One day while talking to a fellow by the name of Dick Mace, who runs a wholesale fishing tackle operation in Maryland, I let it be known (in case he had secrets to share) that I was working on a new grilling book. "The best steak I've ever grilled had bourbon on it," he said.

"Oh?" Silence on the line. "How did you cook it, Dick?" I asked.

"I grilled it," he said.

"Well . . . did you have a marinade or did you just pour the bourbon over the steak?"

"To tell you the truth," he said, "I really don't remember."

Well, I suppose that some of the best dishes ever cooked are forever lost because the creator doesn't remember, for one reason or another, the list of ingredients or the particulars. Perhaps the good flavor of the following recipe will jog Dick's memory:

New York strip steaks	**1 tablespoon fresh lemon**
½ cup good bourbon	**juice**
¼ cup firmly packed	**1 tablespoon**
brown sugar	**Worcestershire sauce**
¼ cup water	**1 tablespoon garlic powder**
5 ounces soy sauce	**salt and pepper to taste**

Mix the bourbon, water, soy sauce, lemon juice, Worcestershire sauce, garlic powder, and brown sugar, stirring well. Put the steaks into a plastic Ziploc bag and pour the marinade mixture over them. Marinate in the refrigerator for 8 hours, turning the bag from time to time.

Build a medium hot fire and adjust the rack to about 5 inches from the coals. When the coals have burned down, drain the meat and put the marinade into your basting pot. Grill the steaks for 4 to 6 minutes on each side for medium rare, or until done the way you like them. Baste the meat several times with the marinade liquid while cooking. Serve hot, with salt and pepper to taste.

Island Teriyaki

This is a favorite Hawaiian dish calling for beefsteak that has been cut into thin strips, marinated in soy sauce, and grilled over hot coals. Here's what you'll need:

> **2 pounds of tender beefsteak**
> **½ cup soy sauce**
> **1 tablespoon freshly ground ginger root or ½**
>   **tablespoon powdered ginger**
> **3 cloves garlic, minced**
> **1 medium onion, chopped**
> **½ cup saké or sherry**

Using a sharp knife, cut the steak into strips about ¼-inch thick. Mix the soy sauce, ginger, garlic, onion, and saké (or sherry). Put the steak into a glass container, pour the sauce over it, stir to coat all sides, and marinate for 2 hours. Build a hot fire in your grill and adjust the racks about 4 inches above the coals. Thread each strip of meat in an S-shape onto skewers and cook quickly over the coals for several minutes on each side. Do not overcook. Serve hot with white rice.

Note: A similar teriyaki is also popular in Japanese cuisine, where the meat is often (but not always) stir-fried instead of grilled. It is cut into thin strips so that it can be eaten easily with chopsticks. The steak is easier to cut into strips if you put it into the freezer until the meat is almost frozen. In some variations, the steak is first cooked in a rather large piece, then cut into strips before it is served.

Also in the Orient, small strips of marinated meat are cooked at a wooden dining table on a charcoal grill. Each person cooks his own meat, using long chopsticks to handle the strips. I call the technique "Mongolian fondue" because it probably came from the steppes of Mongolia and down through China. (In a similar cooking technique, the Mongols boiled small strips of meat in a sauce of some sort, using a Mongolian Hot Pot, which is a cooking device with a container for charcoal and a built-in pot for the liquid.) Remember, however, that the Mongols of the steppes usually lived in large round tents (yurts), which had a vent hole in the top. Unless you live in a yurt or teepee or igloo, you might consider holding your Mongolian fondue party outside on the patio table.

GRILLING LAMB AND GOAT

The meat of lamb has a flavor all its own, which is intensified in the larger mutton. The meat is often marinated before it is cooked over coals, as in the popular kabobs of the Middle East. Personally, I love the flavor of grilled lamb, and I prefer to keep the marinade simple. Those people who think that they do not care for lamb should trim all the fat from it, or cook it in such a way that the fat doesn't drip onto hot coals.

In some sections of the world, lamb is not a common meat. Not a single supermarket or meat house in the county where I live stocks lamb at all. In a larger town nearby (Dothan, Alabama) lamb is sometimes available, but the selection is usually quite limited. A few farmers in the area have sheep, but most don't care for the meat. Or think they don't. Nonetheless, it is possible to buy a whole lamb (or mutton) and butcher it yourself or take it to a meat processor. Lamb is usually more readily available in other parts of the world, and even dominates the cookery in Iran and some other areas. In addition to the popular lamb chop and the kabob, the meat of lamb is often cooked in such a dish as Irish stew. In some areas, mutton is just as popular as lamb, but it is not widely marketed in the United States, although it is widely available in Canada. Of course, sheep, having lots of fleece, fare better in colder climates. It is really not an important meat in Mexico, where the short-haired goat does better.

Goat meat is often eaten in the Mediterranean countries and in some parts of Latin America. In the United States it is even harder to find in markets than lamb, although it (or at least kid) may be available in Greek or Caribbean markets. Yet, goats are still raised on farms in North America, and buying one whole is seldom a problem if you ask around. My advice is to select a young nanny goat (or a male that has been cut) and butcher it yourself, making certain that it is not riled up at the moment of slaughter. High adrenaline levels will make the meat strong. It's also best to hang the meat in a cooler for a week or longer after butchering. In general, if in doubt, select a young goat or kid.

The goat, like the sheep, has a white fat that should be removed before direct grilling. Because the fat doesn't smell good when it drips onto the hot coals, most people of my acquaintance cook the meat by indirect cooking or by wrapping it in aluminum foil, or both. I've also eaten some wonderful goat that was wrapped in burlap and slowly cooked in a pit, as described in Part Five.

When grilling goat for the first time, it's best, I think, to cut out the back strap, then butterfly it, making boneless loin chops about ¾ inch thick. This will give you a choice, tender piece of meat that has very little fat. If you like the flavor of the goat, proceed with the leg and the shoulder. Or try the whole goat, cooked very, very slowly. In Saudi Arabia, goats are stuffed and roasted whole over charcoal.

In any case, I am not offering a specific goat recipe here, but, as a rule, a young goat or kid can be cooked with any of the lamb recipes.

Lamb Chops

Here's one of my favorite recipes for lamb. For direct grilling, I like to have chops that are 1½ inches thick.

> **lamb chops**
> **olive oil**
> **garlic**
> **fresh parsley or thyme**
> **salt and pepper to taste**

Build a good fire in the grill and adjust the rack to about 8 inches above the coals. (Remember that lamb, unlike beefsteak, profits from rather slow grilling.) Crush the garlic and add it to the olive oil, then stir in chopped parsley (or thyme). Pour the marinade over the lamb chops in a bowl. I don't have exact measures to offer, but all you need do is coat all sides of the chops with the marinade. When the fire is right, grill for 7 or 8 minutes on each side. Baste once or twice with any remaining marinade. During the last minute or two, sprinkle both sides of the meat with salt and pepper to taste. Do not overcook. The meat should be crispy on the outside and pink on the inside.

Variations: Lamb is often served with mint jelly, and I sometimes add a few crushed mint leaves to the marinade. I have also made a basting sauce of butter and crushed mint leaves, heated in a saucepan. Although mint sauce and such sweet stuff as pepper jelly are eaten with lamb, a spicy tomato-based sauce also goes good with the meat. See the recipe for Moroccan Kabobs, page 95. Also try the following mint sauce:

> **⅔ cup mint jelly**
> **⅓ cup lemon juice**
> **¼ cup fresh mint leaves, minced**
> **2 tablespoons butter**

Melt the butter in a small saucepan, then stir in the other ingredients and simmer until the jelly melts. Do not boil. Put the sauce into a serving bowl and spoon it directly onto the fully cooked lamb.

Sosaties

This is a festive dish, served at *braaivleis,* or outdoor cookouts, in the south of Africa. I normally cook the dish with lamb, as specified in the recipe, but I suspect that the dish is very old and might well have been used with monkey or some other good meat. In any case, try it with lamb, mutton, or kid goat. The recipe called for sticking the meat on skewers (sometimes with lamb fat between the pieces) but I usually cook it with pieces larger than are normally used on kabobs. If you use chunks, you can always put them into a hinged basket, as I do.

3 pounds lamb
4 medium onions, peeled
 and minced
I clove garlic
½ cup fresh lemon juice
¼ cup peanut oil
2 tablespoons apricot
 jam
I tablespoon dark brown
 sugar

I ½ teaspoons ground
 coriander
I teaspoon hot curry
 powder (see below)
½ teaspoon ground cumin
2 bay leaves or fresh
 lemon leaves
2 tablespoons flour
salt and pepper
½ cup water

Split the garlic clove, then rub it over the lamb. Cut the lamb into pieces and sprinkle with salt and pepper to taste. Place the meat in a glass or nonmetallic bowl. Heat the oil in a skillet and sauté the onions until they are golden. Stir in the coriander, cumin, and hot curry powder. (To make hot curry powder, add ⅛ teaspoon of cayenne pepper to ordinary curry powder.) Simmer for 3 minutes, then add the brown sugar, lemon juice, and apricot jam. Turn up the heat, stir in ½ cup water, and bring to a quick boil, stirring constantly with a wooden spoon. After it boils, remove the sauce from the heat and let stand. When it is cool, pour the sauce over the meat, sticking in the bay or lemon leaves. Cover and refrigerate for 12 hours or longer.

When you are ready to cook, build a good fire and let it burn down until you have hot coals. Put the meat into a hinged basket or thread it onto skewers, then cook it for 15 minutes or longer, depending on how thick the chunks are. While the meat is cooking, remove the leaves from the sauce. Put the sauce into a cast-iron skillet and bring to a bubble. Slowly stir in the flour, using a wooden spoon, until the sauce is thick. Remove from the heat and pour it into a serving dish. Keep it warm until the meat is ready.

The measures in this recipe will serve 6 hungry people, maybe 8, depending on what else you've got to eat. Traditionally, this dish is served with rice that has been colored yellow with turmeric or saffron.

Butterflied Leg of Lamb

As any hungry man who has taken a look at lamb chops will agree, the regular cuts of meat from a lamb are quite small as compared to beef or even pork. The shoulder of lamb, as usually cut by commercial butchers, is a complicated piece of meat containing part of the backbone and ribs as well as the front leg. It is a very good piece of meat, but not too well-suited for direct grilling. The leg of lamb usually weighs 8 or 9 pounds, and is often roasted. It is highly recommended for indirect cooking, as discussed in Part Three. If you want a good-size chunk of meat for direct grilling, try a butterflied leg of lamb. First, bone the meat, then spread the meat open. This will give you a continuous piece of meat that weighs about 6 pounds. It will, however, be thicker and broader on one end. Cooking it directly over coals can yield a piece of meat that is well done on one end and rare on the other. If you want all the meat cooked to the same doneness, try tilting a grid over the fire so that the thick part is closer to the heat. With the aid of several bricks, I can usually rig some such tilted grill in my kitchen fireplace or in a campfire built on the ground.

> **leg of lamb, boned and butterflied**
> **1 cup olive oil**
> **juice of 3 large onions** (see below)
> **juice of 2 lemons**
> **½ tablespoon marjoram**
> **2 bay leaves, crushed**
> **salt and pepper to taste**

Bone and butterfly the lamb. Cut the onions into chunks of suitable size and squeeze out the juice with the aid of a garlic press. Mix oil, onion juice, lemon juice, marjoram, and bay leaves. Put the lamb into a suitable nonmetallic container and pour the marinade over it, turning to coat all sides. (Or use a large plastic bag.) Refrigerate the lamb overnight, turning once or twice. When you are ready to cook, rig the grid for tilted cooking (about 30 degrees), as described above. It's best to have the thick part at least 8 inches from the heat. Grill over medium-hot coals for a total of 15 minutes on each side, turning every 5 minutes or so. Brush lightly with a little olive oil. Toward the end of the cooking time, salt and pepper both sides to taste.

GRILLING PORK

Pork is a choice meat for the grill, but remember that fresh pork must be well done to be eaten safely. Some authorities recommend that it be cooked long enough to reach an internal temperature of 185 degrees. Others go down to 140 degrees. I usually settle for about 160 degrees for larger pieces of meat. Chops and thin cuts don't cause much of a problem, and I cook them until no reddish juice runs out when they are cut. Further, pork doesn't suffer as much in flavor when it is cooked well done, although some of the best cuts—such as tenderloin—will tend to dry out. Some of the larger cuts of pork, such as the Boston butt, are best suited for indirect cooking, smoking, or pit barbecue. These are discussed in other parts of this book. The recipes below work nicely for direct grilling close to the coals on either an open grill or in a covered grill.

Pork Tenderloin & Grilled Potatoes

In order to make larger pieces, pork tenderloin can be sliced and butterflied. I usually make mine about ½-inch thick and grill them quickly over hot coals. Thicker pieces should be grilled for a longer time and at a greater distance from the coals, so that the inside will get done before the outside chars. Untrimmed pork chops should also be grilled farther from the fire, simply because they contain lots of fat that drips badly and causes flare-ups when grilled too close to the heat.

The potatoes that I usually grill with this recipe can be of most any sort. I prefer the smaller red potatoes, but I have also used large baking potatoes, sliced lengthwise. The potatoes should be cut into ½-inch slices. Leave the skin on.

pork tenderloin
Italian salad dressing
potatoes

Cut the tenderloin into butterfly pieces ½-inch thick. (Pork loin is wider than tenderloin, so cut it into wheels.) Put the meat into a nonmetallic container and pour some Italian salad dressing over it, stirring about to coat all sides. Or use a plastic Ziploc bag.

Build a fire while the pork marinates. Adjust the grid to about 4 inches above the coals. After the coals are ready, slices the potatoes ½-inch thick and put them onto the grid. Baste the potatoes with some of the Italian salad dressing. When the potatoes have cooked for 4 or 5 minutes, arrange the pork pieces on the grid beside the potato slices. Cook for 4 or 5 minutes, then turn and baste both the potatoes and the pork. Cut into a piece of the pork to make sure that it is done all the way through. Do not overcook. Take up the pork. Baste the potatoes, then test a slice with a fork. If tender, take them up. (The potatoes should also be slightly browned on the outside, but not burned.) Serve with lots of tossed salad.

Note: The Italian salad dressing used in this recipe is clear, consisting of oil, vinegar, and spices. Do not use the creamy dressings. Pork tenderloin is low in fat, but the Italian salad dressing itself is rather high in calories. Use a "light" dressing if you prefer.

Grilled Pepper Ham & Pineapple

Although some of the "cured" hams for sale in today's supermarkets are said to be fully cooked, I still prefer to grill or broil the meat before eating it. Most of these hams are pumped full of water, and I like to get it out. One of my favorite ways to prepare ham steaks is to grill them over a hot charcoal fire, very close to the coals, for a few minutes on each side. The best steak for grilling, of course, is the center cut. These can be purchased separately, or you can have them cut from the center of a whole ham. In any case, they should be at least ½-inch thick. (Thicker ham steaks, say 2 inches, should be cooked farther from the coals and for a longer period of time. See the next recipe.)

Cured ham is good when cooked without any sort of seasoning added to it, but I like lots of coarse black pepper on mine, and some mustard. Although I specify Dijon-style mustard, most any sort of prepared mustard will work.

The pineapple that I cook with this dish is fresh, and I cut it lengthwise into quarters—top, peeling, core, and all. Thus, each piece has two flat sides and I rounded side with the peeling. First I put one flat side down onto the grill, and then the other. The peeling side is never face down to the heat.

ham steak
freshly ground pepper
Dijon mustard
fresh pineapple

When you are ready to cook, build a good charcoal fire. While the coals burn down, grind some pepper. Spread some mustard onto each side of the ham steak and sprinkle on a little pepper. Quarter the pineapple. When the coals are right, put the steak onto the grid and arrange the pineapple quarters around it. Leaving the stem end attached to the pineapple quarters makes it easy to turn and handle them during cooking. After 6 or 7 minutes, turn the ham steaks and the pineapple. Cook for another 6 minutes, or until the ham starts to brown nicely. Do not overcook. The pineapple should be hot and slightly browned on the outside when the ham is ready to take up.

With a sharp knife, cut off the top core part of each piece of pineapple, then run your knife between the skin and the fruit. Slice the fruit into 1-inch segments, so that it can be eaten with a fork. Leave the pieces on the peeling, which acts as a serving boat.

51

Grilled Ham Roast

My grocer markets a thick slice of meat cut from the center of a precooked cured ham. He calls it a "roast," as compared to a thinner cut, which he calls a "steak." His roasts are from 2½ to 3½ inches thick. (Note: Thinner cuts of ham can be cooked much more quickly than thick cuts. See the previous recipe.) My family is very fond of the thicker cuts, which I always serve on an oblong platter, topped with grilled sliced pineapple. I also use the juice from a can of pineapple in the recipe.

I thick piece of center-cut ham, precooked
I small can sliced pineapple
I teaspoon powdered mustard
I teaspoon white pepper

¼ cup pineapple juice (from the can)
¼ cup red wine vinegar
¼ cup olive oil
¼ cup soy sauce
½ teaspoon ground cloves or cinnamon

Mix the red wine vinegar, soy sauce, olive oil, pineapple juice, mustard, white pepper, and ground cloves (or cinnamon). Put the ham into an oblong dish and pour the sauce over it. Marinate for I hour or longer, turning once or twice.

Build a charcoal fire (or heat up the gas or electric grill) and adjust the racks to about 8 inches from the coals. Put the ham on a grid and cook it for 30 minutes, turning and basting from time to time. Lower the grid to within 4 inches of the coals and put the slices of pineapple on the grid beside the ham. Turn both ham and pineapple after a few minutes. Baste the ham and pineapple. Continue to turn and baste every few minutes, or until the ham is nicely browned, showing char spots here and there. Remove the ham to a serving platter and arrange the pineapple slices on top.

Allow about ¼ pound of ham per person. Heavy eaters may eat ½ pound, but, generally, ham is filling and goes further than beef. Leftover ham can be sliced, warmed in a skillet, and eaten with hot biscuits for breakfast.

Country Ribs

These cuts of meat and bone, which come from the top of the backbone instead of from the rib cage, are more meaty than true ribs. They are, however, a little too fatty for direct grilling close to the coals. For this reason, I recommend that they be baked in the oven, then transferred to the grill. Here's all you need:

> **country ribs** (¾ pound per person)
> **red wine vinegar**
> **salt and pepper**
> **cinnamon**

Sprinkle the ribs with red wine vinegar and set aside for 1 hour. Preheat the oven to 350 degrees F. Put the ribs on a rack in a pan and bake for 40 minutes. Shortly after putting the ribs into the oven, build a hot fire in the grill and adjust the rack to about 3 inches from the coals. After baking the ribs in the oven, baste them with the pan drippings, then sprinkle both sides with salt, pepper, and cinnamon.

Grill for 4 or 5 minutes on each side, basting two or three times with the liquid from the pan and adding a little salt, pepper, and cinnamon. Go light on the cinnamon. Serve the ribs with potato salad.

Barbecue Variation: Proceed as above. After taking the ribs out of the oven, baste them with a thick tomato-based barbecue sauce. Grill at a distance of 5 or 6 inches from the coals for a total of 6 or 7 minutes on each side, turning and basting lightly every 3 minutes.

Honey Chops

For this recipe, I want rather lean pork about ½-inch thick. Although I usually buy loin chops or T-bone pork chops, I also like to purchase a tenderloin of pork and butterfly it into ½-inch pieces.

pork chops or tenderloin
prepared mustard
honey
lemon-pepper seasoning salt

Rinse the chops and put them into a suitable nonmetallic dish. Sprinkle both sides lightly with lemon-pepper, then brush both sides lightly with prepared mustard. I prefer to use the brown Creole-style mustard, but Dijon or ordinary yellow mustard will do. Leave the chops at room temperature for at least 30 minutes.

Build a hot charcoal fire (or heat your electric or gas unit.) Using tongs, place the chops on the rack about 4 inches above the coals. Grill for 8 minutes on each side, turning once. Brush one side with honey and sprinkle with lemon pepper. Grill the side with honey for 2 minutes, then brush the other side with honey, sprinkle with lemon pepper, and grill for 2 minutes.

Note: I like the taste of mustard with fresh pork, and I use quite a bit of it on the chops that I grill for myself. The first time or two that you cook this recipe, it's probably wise to use thin coats of mustard on most of the meat, then try one piece with a heavy coat. This will help determine your preference.

GRILLING CHICKEN AND OTHER BIRDS

Large pieces of chicken are not difficult to cook on a grill, but all too often the outside gets done while there's still red blood around the bones. Nothing kills a dinner quicker, in my experience, than bloody chicken. This culinary sin isn't limited to the jackleg patio chef, either. Experienced kitchen cooks and even restaurant chefs sometimes err in this direction.

Not long ago, for example, a home economics expert came to our town to demonstrate an electric patio grill for a company that she worked for. She cooked outside on the sidewalk. The chicken was bloody, even though she had cooked the recipe several times in their test facilities and thought that she had the timing down pat. But she was done in, and highly embarrassed, by bloody chicken. What happened? A high wind came up, and, I think, she took the lid off the smoker too often to show the insides to passersbyers.

In any case, thick pieces of chicken are even more difficult to cook to perfection by grilling them over charcoal. The trick is to put the meat a good 8 inches above the coals—and have patience. Just the other night, I had to grill some large chicken breasts (not boned) for well over an hour before they were right. By right, I mean that they were juicy inside (but didn't have much red liquid around the bone) and crispy on the outside. In this case, I recommend that any patio chef master the technique on an open grill, even though he may have covered grills or other means of indirect cooking. After all, the uncovered grills are available in parks and campgrounds, and are easily improvised over a campfire. Further, I am certain that the technique of grilling chicken is far more important than the recipe, provided that you have good meat. In any case, here is a simple recipe that I use often:

Grilled Chicken Quarters

I feel that most people put too much emphasis on marinades for chicken. The truth is that the fryers and broilers that are normally purchased in supermarkets and other outlets are quite tender and need no tenderizing marinade. All you need in order to grill tasty chicken is a little seasoning salt—and patience. But I do often use a combination quick marinade and basting sauce, as indicated below:

1 chicken
½ cup soy sauce
½ cup Worcestershire sauce
pepper

If you dress your own chicken, split it in half, then separate the leg quarter from the breast. Cut off the wings and save them along with the giblets. Mix the soy sauce, Worcestershire sauce, and black pepper. In a nonmetallic container, coat the chicken and marinate it for at least ½ hour, while the charcoal fire is getting right.

Put the rack about 8 inches over the coals, then grill the chicken for 10 minutes. Turn and baste. Grill for another 10 minutes. Turn and baste. From then on, turn and baste the chicken every 5 minutes and cook until done. A small chicken may take less than 40 minutes, and a large chicken may take over an hour. A good deal will depend on how hot the fire is. In any case, I usually cook mine until I am sure than it is done, turning frequently toward the end. I usually cut a piece all the way to the bone before serving it.

While the chicken is cooking, I suggest that you use the chicken wings and giblets to make a pilaf. In a pan with a tight lid, bring to boil 3½ cups of water along with ⅓ teaspoon of red pepper flakes and 1 teaspoon of salt. Add the chicken pieces, cover, and boil until the gizzard is tender. Bone the meat and chop the gizzard, heart, and liver. Put the meat and chopped giblets back into the pot and turn up the heat. Add 1 cup of long-grain rice, bring to a boil, reduce heat, cover tightly, and let simmer for 20 minutes. Leave the cover off and simmer until the texture is right for eating with a fork without dripping. Serve the pilaf along with the broiled chicken, vegetables, salad, and bread.

If you prefer not to fool with the pilaf, I still recommend that you cut the wings off the breast quarters. When cooked along with the rest of the chicken, the wings get done much quicker and can be used as appetizers by for the guests or as a chef's reward.

A. D.'s Fireplace Chicken Thighs

My favorite piece of chicken for the fireplace grill is the thigh, although wings can be mighty tasty. Skinning the thighs eliminates lots of fat, which can drip down and start fires in your coals and make your chicken taste like burnt grease. Removing the skin, however, causes the meat to dry out, so that it requires constant attention, or at least frequent turning and basting. In any case, here is all you need to cook tasty chicken in the fireplace or on an open grill:

> **chicken thighs**
> **apple cider vinegar**
> **lemon-pepper seasoning salt**

Put the chicken thighs in a glass bowl and pour a little vinegar over them. Sprinkle with lemon-pepper seasoning. Cover and put into the refrigerator for several hours, stirring from time to time. When you are ready to cook, build a good fire and set the chicken thighs out. Skin the thighs and put them back into the marinade container. When the coals are ready, place the chicken, spaced tightly, onto the rack directly over the coals. Set a container of apple cider vinegar and a bottle of lemon-pepper on the hearth where it will be handy to the grill. You will also need a basting brush and tongs. Cook the chicken for 5 minutes, then turn it and cook on the other side for 5 minutes. Turn the chicken and baste lightly with vinegar, then sprinkle lightly with lemon-pepper. Repeat this process, turning, basting, and sprinkling every 5 minutes.

When the chicken is done, it will have shrunk considerably in volume and will be quite brown on the outside. If in doubt, have a knife and saucer at hand for cutting into a piece from time to time. The first time you cook this dish, remember that the lemon-pepper contains both salt and pepper. Use it sparingly until you gain experience, and then increase it to suit your taste.

Grilled Quail Alexandria

According to Claudia Roden's work, *A Book of Middle Eastern Food,* large numbers of migrating quail are netted each year on the beaches near Alexandria and cooked over fires built in the sand. (This tradition goes back to Biblical times, when quail, exhausted from the flight across the Mediterranean, were captured with a weighted blanket.) I've never had the good fortune to feast on migrating quail, but I have tried the Egyptian recipe on wild American bobwhites as well as on pen-raised quail that I buy freshly dressed from a local farmer or frozen from my grocer.

The onion juice and other ingredients in the marinade sauce in this recipe are just right. The measures below provide plenty of marinade for 8 quail. (The butter is my own addition and was not in the original.) If this dish is to be served as an entrée, you'll need at least 2 birds per person. I'll take a few more, if you've got them.

8 quail	I teaspoon ground cumin
I large onion	I teaspoon ground
2 tablespoons finely	coriander
chopped fresh parsley,	salt and cayenne pepper to
or I tablespoon dried	taste
¼ cup olive oil	butter, melted (optional)

When dressing the quail for this recipe, I pluck them, remove the innards, and cut them in half. Usually, wild meat is better after it has seasoned for a few days in the refrigerator, but quail really doesn't require this curing. I often eat birds that have been frozen, and I much prefer that quail, doves, and similar birds be frozen under water in a milk carton.

When your birds are ready, peel the onion, quarter it, and squeeze out the juice with a garlic press. Mix onion juice, oil, parsley, cumin, coriander, salt, and cayenne pepper. (Remember that cayenne pepper is really hot stuff.) After the mixture has steeped for a while, rub the birds with it inside and out. Then place the birds in a suitable glass container and pour the sauce over them. Marinade for I hour or 2, turning once or twice. Build a hot fire with the grid about 4 inches from the heat. Grill the bird halves for 5 or 6 minutes on each side, or until done. I usually baste mine with hot melted butter when they are almost ready to take up, then I grill them for a minute or so on each side.

Note: This is an excellent recipe for camp, in case you are lucky enough to bag your own birds. The marinade can be mixed at home and carried in a suitable spice jar.

Barbecued Chicken

This method for cooking chicken can be used with any good sauce. Remember, however, that most of the commercial barbecue sauces have a thick tomato base, and should be used only after the chicken is almost done. In other words, grill the chicken for a good while before swabbing on a thick tomato-based sauce. If you want a different flavor, however, experiment with other sauces, or try the one below. Such sauces, thinner than most tomato-based barbecue pastes, can be basted onto the meat all during the cooking, not just at the end. I like both kinds, however. To the sauce below, I add the brown sugar toward the end of the grilling, since it also tends to burn with long cooking.

2 broiler chickens
½ cup margarine
½ cup red wine vinegar
¼ cup Worcestershire sauce
½ tablespoon paprika

½ teaspoon prepared mustard
I teaspoon salt
½ teaspoon Tabasco sauce
I tablespoon brown sugar

Build a good charcoal in your grill fire and let it burn down. Adjust the rack to about 8 inches above the coals. Split the chickens lengthwise. Trim off the excess fat from the rear end, but do not skin the birds. Melt the margarine in your basting pot, then mix in the other ingredients except for the brown sugar. Be sure to keep the sauce warm; you'll be adding the brown sugar later. Grease the grid and put the birds on, skin side down. Baste lightly. Cook for 15 minutes, basting twice. Turn and cook for another 15 minutes, basting several times. Turn and baste every 5 minutes until the birds are done. For the last 10 minutes of cooking time, I mix the brown sugar into the warm basting sauce, then baste thickly on both sides of the chicken. I allow I hour to cook the birds, give or take 5 minutes either way. To test for doneness, you can either poke on the flesh with your finger, stick a fork into the breast, or twist the legs around—but it's best to cut into the thickest part of one piece (your own) before serving. Most of us like our chicken well done but not dry. I allow half a chicken per person, served directly from the grill onto plates.

For more barbecue inspiration, see Part Five.

Chicken Mozambique

This recipe is quite similar to Prawns Mozambique, but coconut milk is used instead of lemon juice. I have cooked this chicken dish several times, and I usually use skinned thighs instead of breasts or other pieces. Sometimes I cook Chicken Mozambique over charcoal in my hearth, as well as on the patio.

3 to 4 pounds of chicken thighs, skinned
½ cup peanut oil
8 hot peppers, or 4 teaspoons of red pepper flakes
2 cups coconut milk
4 cloves garlic, crushed
½ cup chopped fresh parsley
½ teaspoon salt

Skin the chicken thighs. Mix the peppers (or red pepper flakes), coconut milk, parsley, garlic, and salt. Pour the ½ of the mixture over the chicken and marinate 2 hours or longer in a nonmetallic bowl. (Save the remaining sauce.)

Build the hot fire in a grill and let the coals burn down. Warm the oil and mix in the remaining sauce. Place the chicken on a rack over the hot coals. Cook for 10 minutes on one side, turn and baste with the heated sauce. Cook the other side for 10 minutes, basting once or twice. Then turn and baste ever few minutes until the chicken is done all the way to the bone. The exact cooking time will depend on how hot your fire is, on how close the chicken is to it, and on how large the pieces are.

If you have basting sauce left over, pour it into a small bowl and serve it with the chicken.

Note: Chicken breasts tend to dry out considerably when cooking directly over hot coals. If you use breasts, consider leaving the skin on them. I have cooked chicken halves (with the skin on) by pretty much the same method as above, but more often than not I use a large hooded grill and cook the meat very slowly for at least 2 hours.

Rock cornish hens and quail can also be cooked by this recipe. I usually cut these in half and grill them directly over hot coals. Over really hot coals, quail halves need only a few minutes on each side.

Coconut milk is available in some stores. It is easy to make your own from either freshly shredded or grated coconut meat. To 2 cups of coconut meat, add 2 cups of boiling water. Let this sit for 30 minutes, then strain off the milk. Put the pulp into a piece of cheesecloth and squeeze it in order to get the richest coconut milk. It's best to use freshly grated coconut, but packaged coconut can also be used. Remember that the juice inside a fresh coconut is just that: coconut juice. Real coconut milk is made from the meat.

Thai Garlic Chicken

The recipes used in Thailand, Burma, and other parts of Asia use lots of garlic and coriander. In our own country, coriander has become more and more popular in recent years, especially as used in our version of Mexican cooking, where it is called cilantro. It is available in some markets under the name Chinese parsley or Mexican parsley. Further, it is very easy to grow at home in your herb garden or bay window. Merely sprinkle a few seeds on top of rich dirt, and sprinkle a little dirt over the seeds. Then sprinkle with water. In about three weeks, you'll have coriander plants. In the recipe below, note that the whole plant is used—leaves, stems, and roots—and for best results the plants should be pulled up when they are about 6 inches high. The seeds of coriander are sold whole or ground as a spice, and they are a major ingredient in curry powder.

> **8 chicken breast halves**
> **juice of 2 lemons**
> **6 cloves garlic**
> **20 peppercorns**
> **4 coriander plants, roots and all**
> **2 teaspoons salt**

Wash the coriander and chop it finely. Wash the chicken pieces and cut off large blobs of fat, leaving the skin intact. With a mortar and pestle, crush the peppercorns and grind the garlic cloves. Mix the minced coriander, pepper, garlic, salt, and lemon juice. Rub the mixture into the chicken pieces and leave for 1 hour at room temperature, or longer under refrigeration.

When you are ready to cook, build a fire in your grill and put the chicken pieces over it. For best results, chicken breasts should be cooked slowly. I cook mine about 8 inches above the coals for 8 to 12 minutes on each side. (This cooking time is for boned chicken breast without skin.) Do not cook too long, especially if you use skinned chicken. Remember that skinned chicken breast is dry—and the marinade used above has no oil whatsoever in it.

Serve the chicken with rice and a large tossed salad with lots of ripe tomato chunks in it.

Variation: If you don't have coriander at hand, try substituting ½ cup of fresh parsley, very finely chopped, along with a touch of grated horseradish or prepared horseradish. It won't be the same as the Thai dish, but it will be very good.

Rock Cornish Hens

These birds, when halved, grill nicely over direct heat, with the rack about 6 inches from the coals. They are small enough to cook through in a reasonable time, and large enough to eat easily, if you use your fingers. I always allow one bird per person, but half a bird might do for very light eaters.

> **rock Cornish game hens**
> **½ cup olive oil**
> **¼ white wine Worcestershire sauce**
> **juice of 1 lemon**
> **zest of 1 lemon**
> **salt and white pepper**

The measures above will work for 3 or 4 hens. Increase marinade measures for cooking a larger batch. Split the game hens in half and sprinkle with salt and white pepper. Mix the oil, white wine Worcestershire sauce, lemon juice, and zest. Put the game hen halves in a nonmetallic container and pour the marinade over it. (Or use a plastic Ziploc bag.) Turn to coat all sides of the meat. Marinate for 2 hours.

With the rack about 6 inches over the coals, grill the hens for 25 or 30 minutes, or until done. Turn and baste several times while cooking.

Grilled Cider Duckling

Wild ducks vary considerably in size from the tiny teal to a plumb cornfed mallard. The flavor of the meat depends in large part on what the duck has been eating and on proper field dressing. By comparison, the large domestic ducks that are available on the market hold few surprises. They are all large, fat, and delicious when properly prepared. They are a little tricky to grill, however, partly because of fat content. I normally use the breast fillets for direct grilling, saving the rest for duck soup or gumbo. Or for smoking. But I have cooked leg quarters (including the thigh) by direct grilling, and found the meat to be quite good. The technique set forth above for similar cuts of chicken will work, although you may want to vary the marinade and baste. Actually, domestic duck doesn't require much seasoning, and you can get by nicely with a sprinkling of celery salt.

For direct grilling, I prefer the duck breasts with the fatty skin left on. It may not be good for your cholesterol level, but it sure is tasty. Here's what you'll need:

> **fillets of duck breast**
> **apple cider**
> **salt and pepper**

Bone the duck breast and score the skin side, making shallow cuts into the fat and forming a diamond lattice. Put the fillets into a glass container and cover with apple cider. Marinate for 8 or 10 hours before cooking. When the fire is ready, salt and pepper the ducks lightly and grill about 8 inches above the heat. Turn every 10 minutes, brushing from time to time with the leftover marinade cider. When the breasts are almost done, lower the rack and grill (skin down) very close to the coals until the skin browns on the surface and turns crisp.

I usually allow two fillets per person. But the meat is very rich, and one will be enough for some people. Serve with wild rice and asparagus.

Birds David Hicks

A civil engineer by the of name David Hicks cooks on a kettle-shaped grill with a missing top. He said that the top blew away while he was hauling the grill in the back his pickup truck. Aerodynamics, pure and simple. But he improvised a hood with a large sheet of extra-heavy aluminum foil, which he felt did an even better job than the store-bought hood in retaining the convective heat. "It probably reflects the radiant heat better, too," he said. Thermodynamically it probably does.

In any case, his grilled doves are quite tasty. The recipe will also work with breast of snipe, woodcock, and quail. Marsh hens may require a soak in a marinade made of 1 or 2 tablespoons of baking soda to a quart of water.

> **dove breasts**
> **butter**
> **bacon**
> **celery salt**
> **pepper**

Pluck the bird breasts instead of skinning them. Carefully slit each breast on each side of the breastbone with a thin knife. Sprinkle each bird lightly with celery salt and pepper, inside the slits and out.

When you are ready to cook, build a medium-hot fire in your grill. When the coals burn down just right, put a thin slice of butter into the slit on either side of the breastbone of each bird. Then wrap the breast with half a strip of bacon and pin with round toothpicks. Put the bird breasts onto the grill, about 4 inches from the heat. Cover. Grill for 5 minutes, then turn the birds, close the hood, and grill the other side for 5 minutes. Cook each side a little longer, as needed.

Hicks says that the birds will be done when the bacon looks ready to eat. Damned if they aren't, if you've got small birds such as doves. Pheasant, grouse, and Cornish game hens should be moved farther away from the heat and cooked for a longer time so that the inside will get done. If in doubt, cut into one before serving the whole batch.

GRILLING FISH & SEAFOOD

Some of the best fish for grilling are rather oily and have flesh that doesn't flake too easily, such as the swordfish and the king mackerel and the amberjack. The meat doesn't dry out quickly, and the fillets or steaks can be turned over without breaking apart. Many of these favorites for the grill should be available at your local fish market.

But more and more of us who enjoy cooking part of our catch are learning that fish with delicate white flesh can also be grilled to perfection. I'm talking about largemouth bass, walleye, crappie, and even bluegill. Happily for the angler, backyard chefs across the land are finding out that some of our favorite sportfish and panfish are even better when cooked on the grill instead of in the skillet. It's true that properly fried walleye fillets or river-run channel catfish are hard to beat for flavor and crunch. But these days we are constantly reminded that eating too much fried fare, no matter how good, may be of coronary consequence.

Tommy Murphy's Basket of Bluegills

A local sport of my acquaintance gave me this recipe when, at a social gathering, I made the statement that large bluegills aren't fit to eat. He laughed, saying that he didn't know what I meant by "large," but that the 1-pound bluegills caught from his pond and cooked in a wire basket on his grill have no strong taste at all. I argued his recipe out of him. The next day I bought one of the rectangular wire baskets at my local barbecue headquarters and headed for the nearest creek. Before sundown, I came back with a batch of assorted bluegills, shellcrackers, and similar "bream." I didn't have a really big one in the bunch, but, on the other hand, all of them were bigger than lima beans. These small fish cooked up just right. Later, I tried the same recipe on some 1-pound crappie, and they too were great. The only difference in technique was that the larger fish required a longer cooking time.

Murphy won't give out the location of the fishing hole that provides ample basketfuls of large bluegills, but here is his secret on how to cook them:

bluegills or other good panfish
Tabasco sauce
salt
1 cup light cooking oil
¼ cup fresh lemon juice
¼ cup vinegar
¼ cup Worcestershire sauce

Scale the fish and cut the heads off. When you slit the belly, make the cut go on past the vent a little toward the tail, exposing some meat, Tommy says. Wash the fish, then put a drop or two of Tabasco sauce in the cavity and on each side. Spread this around the fish with your finger, then sprinkle the fish lightly inside and out with salt.

Build a charcoal fire in the grill, or turn on the gas and heat up the lava rocks, and have the grid about 4 or 5 inches from the heat. In a basting pot, heat the cooking oil, vinegar, lemon juice, and Worcestershire sauce. Keep the sauce warm and handy to the grill.

When your fire is ready, spray the basket with vegetable or other non-stick spray, or brush it with cooking oil. Arrange the fish in the basket. The tails can overlap a bit if necessary, but the thick parts of the fish should barely touch. (Tommy gets 7 bluegills in his basket, and I get about 15 in mine. I didn't ask him the size of his basket. In any case, use two or more baskets if you've got lots of fish.) Adjust the basket to keep the fish tight and lock it shut. Baste both sides of the fish. Put the basket on the grill and cook for about 5 minutes for larger bluegills, or 4 minutes for smaller fare. Baste both sides, turn, and again cook larger fish for 5 minutes or smaller fish for 4 minutes. Baste several times. Turn again. Inspect the fish closely (but don't open the basket yet). When the fish are done, the meat will start pulling away from the backbone. If in doubt, reach through the grid with a fork. If the meat flakes off easily, the fish are done. Open the basket carefully and remove the fish with a spatula.

When done, these fish have a very nice golden brown color. Murphy says that the Worcestershire sauce adds to the color. Maybe it does.

This is a good recipe for camp if you can pack in a long-handled basket. Remember that the basket can be used without a grid over the campfire coals. (In fact, the lid of the basket itself comes in handy as a fine coffee pot grid when placed over a small keyhole fire.) If you don't have bluegill or crappie, try this recipe with any small fish, such as New Hampshire brook trout, Tennessee hornyheads, or California grunion.

Key Lime Barbecue

Most sauces for barbecue have a tomato base. Here's one from the Florida Keys that is different, and quite tasty. It goes well with salt-water fish that have a mild, white flesh, such as dolphin or grouper. It is also very good with such freshwater species as walleye and bass.

> **2 or 3 fish, about 2 pounds each**
> **2 cups brown sugar**
> **½ cup butter or margarine**
> **1 cup fresh lime juice**
> **½ cup soy sauce**
> **salt to taste**

Skin and fillet the fish. To make the marinade and basting sauce, melt the butter (or margarine) and brown sugar in a cast-iron skillet on low heat, then stir in the lime juice and soy sauce. Let the sauce cool somewhat. Put the fillets into a glass or other nonmetallic container and pour the sauce over them. Marinate the fish for 1 hour.

When you are ready to cook, build a charcoal fire (or heat the gas grill) and let it burn down. You'll need only a moderate heat to grill the fillets. Grease the grid so that the fillets won't stick so badly, or, if you prefer, use a hinged basket. Take the fish out of the marinade, then warm the liquid for basting. Place the fillets onto the grill and cook for 5 minutes, basting once. Turn, baste, sprinkle on a little salt if you want it, and cook for 3 or 4 minutes, or until the fish flakes easily when tested with a fork.

Variations: You can also add hickory chips to the charcoal if you want a smoke flavor. Also, larger whole fish of 4 pounds or so can be cooked to advantage by the recipe above. It's best to use a fish-shaped wire basket, put the grid 8 inches or so above the fire, and cook for a much longer period of time. If a whole fish is cooked too close to the fire, the outside will dry out before the inside gets done. It helps to baste the fish often and to turn it several times while it is cooking.

Lazy Boy Grilled Bass

Bass are good for grilling, but they tend to dry out and the fillets tear easily. Here's a recipe that I think solves both problems—while at the same time reducing the time wasted on cleaning the fish. I prefer bass of about 2½ pounds, and I allow a whole fillet per person. To prepare the fish fillets for the grill, run a sharp thin knife behind the dorsal fin and cut along the backbone to the tail. (Or start at the tail and work forward.) Make the same cut on the reverse side. Do not skin or scale the fish.

> **bass fillets (2 or more)**
> **1 large onion**
> **peanut oil**
> **salt to taste**

Build a charcoal fire or heat the gas grill. Prepare the fillets as directed above. Peel the onion, cut it into chunks, and squeeze the juice from it in a garlic press. Mix equal parts of onion juice and oil in a container and warm it.

When the charcoal burns down just right, put the fish, skin down, directly over the coals. (The grid should be at least 4 inches from the heat.) Baste the fish. Close the hood or cover the fish with a tent of aluminum foil. After 5 minutes, baste the fish but do not turn. Close the hood and cook for another 3 minutes. Baste again, sprinkle lightly with salt, and check for doneness by pulling at the meat with a fork; if it tends to flake off, it's ready to eat. Exact cooking times will depend on the thickness of the fish, the fire, how close the fish is to the fire, and so on. Baste and test every 2 or 3 minutes. Overcook at your culinary peril. Take each fillet up with a pancake spatula and place it directly onto serving platters. Eat the fish with the aid of a fork, pulling the meat off the top of the skin and scales.

This recipe will also work with a few wood chips or chunks put beside or on top of the coals. (If you want lots of smoke flavor, however, try the next recipe.)

Although bass is specified in this recipe, it is also a very good method for cooking any good fish that has rather large scales. Also, infinite variations of basting sauce can be used, such as a mixture of 1 part honey and 2 parts mustard. Or brush the fish with melted butter and sprinkle on some salt, lemon-pepper seasoning, and a little onion powder. Or butter and celery salt.

Grilled Fish Steaks

Here's a recipe that can be used with striped bass or any large fish of good flavor. The steaks should be cut to a uniform thickness, which makes them easier to cook the same way. (In my vocabulary, a fish steak is a cross section of the fish, and contains a segment of the backbone.) I recommend that the steaks be cut about 1 inch thick, and that they be grilled about 4 inches from hot coals.

> **fish steaks**
> **butter or margarine**
> **lemon juice**
> **garlic salt**
> **white pepper**
> **mild paprika**
> **salt** (optional)

Moisten each steak on both sides with freshly squeezed lemon juice, then sprinkle lightly with garlic salt and white pepper. After seasoning, stack the steaks on top of each other and let them sit for several hours in the refrigerator.

70

When you are ready to cook, build a charcoal fire in your grill and adjust the rack to about 4 inches from hot coals. Take the steaks out of the refrigerator. When the coals are almost ready, melt about ⅛ inch of butter or margarine in the bottom of a skillet. (People with cholesterol concerns may want to cut back on the butter, or use "light" margarine.) Using tongs, flip-flop each steak in the butter, hold it up to drain quickly, then put it onto the grill. Keep the butter warm in the skillet, and add more if you need it. After 4 minutes, flip flop each steak in butter again and grill the reverse side for 4 minutes. Then sprinkle the steaks (on both sides) lightly with white pepper and rather heavily with a mild paprika. Then grill each side for another minute or two.

It's best to cook this recipe on a grill with a large surface area. Then, in case the dripping butter causes a fire, you can merely move the steaks about with tongs. On a smaller grill, you may want to cut back on the butter, brushing it on instead of dipping the fish into the skillet.

Camp Variation: When you cook breakfast, leave the bacon drippings in the frying pan. If you catch a fish large enough to cut into steaks, you're all set for supper. Warm the bacon grease, flip-flop the steaks in it, sprinkle both sides with lemon-pepper seasoning, and grill over campfire coals for a few minutes on each side. Remember, however, that coals from a campfire are usually much hotter than charcoal, so watch what you are doing unless you like the flavor of burnt fish.

Prawns Mozambique

Prawns are almost identical to large shrimp. They are a little more slender than shrimp, and their average size is between 6 and 7 inches long. If necessary, substitute jumbo shrimp in the recipe below. The larger the prawns or shrimp, the better for this dish. I adapted the recipe from *The Africa News Cookbook,* which recommended that you use very large shrimp that figure less then 10 per pound.

Mozambique has a long coastline on the east side of Africa, where fresh seafood abounds. The country is also noted for its fine open-grill cooking, in which the meat or other fare is cooked directly over coals. Further, Mozambique is also noted for a hot sauce, called Piripiri, which is used as a marinade, as a basting sauce for grilling meat, and as a sauce for use at the table. Putting all this together, I offer the following recipe:

3 or 4 pounds prawns or jumbo shrimp
1 cup peanut oil
8 hot peppers, or 4 teaspoons of red pepper flakes
juice of 4 lemons
4 cloves garlic, minced
½ cup chopped fresh parsley
½ teaspoon salt

Clean the prawns and devein them, but leave the tails in place. These are handy for eating the prawns, and, some say, they add flavor while the meat is being cooked. Mix the peppers (or red pepper flakes), lemon juice, garlic, parsley, and salt. Pour half of the lemon mixture over the prawns and marinate for several hours in a nonmetallic bowl. (Save the other half of the lemon sauce.)

Build the fire in a grill and let the coals burn down. Mix and heat a basting sauce with the rest of the lemon mixture and the oil. Put the peeled prawns on a hot grill about 3 inches from the fire. Cook for 3 to 5 minutes on each side, basting lightly with the heated sauce. (The exact cooking time will depend on how hot your fire is, on how close the prawns are to it, and on how large the prawns are. If in doubt, cut into one of the prawns and check for doneness before serving. The prawn shouldn't be cooked too long.)

Leftover basting mixture can be put into a small bowl and used as a dunking sauce.

Servings: Allow ½ pound of undressed prawns per person, or ⅓ pound of dressed prawns per person. Hearty eaters will demand more.

Note: The peoples of the east coast of Africa have another very hot sauce similar to the one used in the recipe above. It's called Pili Pili, and is made by grinding together (a food processor will work nicely) one pound of hot chilies, I medium onion, a clove of garlic, and the juice of I lemon. Don't get this stuff in your eyes. In fact, it's best to keep it off your hands. A friend of mine in Alabama grows his own peppers and makes a similar sauce from hot peppers. A purist, he doesn't put any lemon or such stuff in it. Red in color, the juice is so strong, some local folks claim, that a drop or two will unclog your kitchen plumbing!

Roasted Oysters

A large grid over coals can be used to roast fresh oysters in the shell. It's simple. Put the oysters on the grill, then stand by with heavy rubber glove, an oyster knife, and a box of crackers. As soon as an oyster pops open, remove it from the grid carefully and finish opening it with the oyster knife, being sure to cut the meat loose from the shell without getting in any grit. (This is something that is learned by experience.) Plop the hot oyster onto a cracker and eat it on the spot. Hurry, before another one pops open. If they stay on the heat very long after popping, the oysters tend to dry out. What you want is a hot, steamed oyster in plenty of the salty liquid. A sauce isn't necessary, but some of us like a drop of hot red sauce with each oyster. The sauce is usually dispensed right out of the bottle, which has a very narrow opening.

James Marker's Grilled Fillet Rolls

This recipe is best cooked with boneless fillets from fish of good size, 5 or 6 pounds, or more. It's best to skin the fillets, then cut them crossways into 1½-inch segments. (Marker says 2 inches, "about like steaks." In my experience, most so-called 2-inch steaks are closer to 1½ inches thick.) In any case, cut all the pieces the same thickness so that the cooking time will be the same.

large fish fillets, skinned
zesty Italian salad dressing
bacon strips
salt (optional)

Put the fish pieces into a nonmetallic container and sprinkle them with zesty Italian salad dressing, coating all sides. Let the fish pieces sit for about 30 minutes. (Marinating the fish too long in too much dressing tends to make them mushy, Marker says.) Build a charcoal fire in your grill, or heat the lava rocks if you use a gas grill. Place the grill about 4 inches from the coals. When you are ready to cook, roll each piece of fish, wrap it with a strip of bacon, and pin it closed with a toothpick. Place the fish over the hot coals and close the hood of your grill. (If your grill doesn't have a hood, make one with a large sheet of aluminum foil. Or try it without a lid if you prefer.) Cook for 7 or 8 minutes, then turn with prongs. Cook for another 7 minutes, or until done. If in doubt, cut into a roll. When it's ready to eat, the flesh will flake easily when tested with a fork. Do not overcook. I like a pinch of salt on mine before serving.

James Marker says that most any kind of fish of suitable size can be cooked by this method. His favorite is snook. I might add that this method is also a very good way to cook fillets from flaky fish, such as largemouth or smallmouth bass. Ordinary fillets from such fish tend to dry out and are hard to turn without flaking.

This recipe is also a good one to cook in camp if you've got a grill or a grid. Or you might try pinning the bacon with a forked stick and holding it over a campfire. A glance at the list of ingredients for this recipe will suggest two other advantages. One, you won't have much stuff to pack into camp. Two, if you don't catch fish, the bacon will provide a bit of meat—and the zesty salad dressing will do wonders for watercress.

GROUND MEAT ON THE GRILL

Once I lived in a pretty town that somehow fielded superior football teams year after year. Good coaches, tradition, community support, a steady crop of athletes with the right stuff, pretty little blond girls to lead the cheer—all of these helped carry the team on to glory. Above all else, however, I credit a few good ol' boy chefs and the great American hamburger. That's right. Hamburgers. Thick and juicy. Hot and tasty. Grilled to perfection.

And the chefs. These fellows, members of the local Quarterback Club, built themselves a long barbecue pit near the concession stand, within view of the main gate. The pit was 12 feet long and about 3 feet wide, and, of course, it was built up waist high for easy reach. Although the pit would burn 12-foot logs, the boys usually fired up only one end of the grill for ordinary ball games. Charcoal provided most of the heat, although they did use quite a bit of green hickory wood for smoke. The smell of the smoke, it was believed, helped sell the burgers, and they wanted enough of it to be seen and smelled from all the way across the field, where the fans of the opposing teams sat.

Further, they cooked burgers all during the game, keeping the smoke going. On a table they had buns and catsup and mustard and large onion slices and tomatoes and lettuce and dill pickles. This table was under the eye and the supervision of the chefs, who would make sure of the supplies and who would lend a helping hand if needed. Near the big grill, the chefs kept some sliced cheese, so that anyone who wanted cheeseburgers would be quickly accommodated. The trick here, of course, was to put a slice of the cheese on a meat patty that was done on one side, so that the cheese would partly melt while the other side was cooking. The chefs also kept a jar of garlic powder at hand for those who wanted stronger fare. The venture was so successful that many of the townspeople started eating at the ball park whenever the team played at home.

The secret of success? These men enjoyed cooking the burgers and took pride in serving up a superior product. To this end, they bought very good meat and put enough of it into the patty. The meat was purchased in bulk, freshly ground by a local meat processor, and the patties were shaped by hand at the ball park. For seasoning, each chef sprinkled a little garlic salt directly onto a handful of meat before shaping it into a patty.

The patties that were ready to eat were stacked to one side of the grill, so that they would stay quite warm but would not dry out from too much heat.

But slowly things changed and un-American activities began to gnaw at the spirit of the thing. By the time my son reached varsity football and I was called upon to lend my services as a chef, the situation had really become hopeless. A new bunch had gained control of the Quarterback Club and one of the duly elected officers fancied himself as something of an efficiency expert. Quite diligently, he put the pencil to all of the operations, made phone calls for the best deals on food stuffs to be sold at the concession stand, and so on. Instead of buying meat in bulk, he reasoned, it would be better to purchase preformed patties. These were much cheaper, and were of a uniform size so that each burger would be exactly the same, thereby saving money in two ways: cheaper meat and less of it.

The guy meant well, and, I'll allow, he spent a considerable amount of his personal time trying to do a good job on saving everybody else time and money. He drove a considerable distance to buy the meat, for example, in spite of the fact that the local schools were trying to persuade everybody to "buy at home" because they were partly dependent upon a county sales tax. He took issue with the buy-at-home plan, at least in the case of the hamburger, saying that the savings were too great to be ignored. It seemed to become a thing of principle. Whether or not the burgers tasted good and sold well never got into the man's figures.

In addition to saving money, he said, the new burgers, thinner and preformed, would also save much time. Therefore, the same number of chefs could cook all the burgers before game time and wouldn't have to cook during the play. The meat could be put into the buns, wrapped with a wax paper napkin, and sold from within the concession stand just like a packaged product. The onions, catsup, and so on could be put on a table out from the concession stand, so that the use of it would not interfere with traffic. All this would save time. I tried to tell the guy that, in this case, time was not money, since all of us volunteered our services, and that I, for one, would prefer to cook a good hamburger the way that I wanted to cook it.

I also tried to tell the guy that his method really wouldn't save time. Trying to separate these frozen patties would take more time than forming your own. And if you let them thaw out before trying to separate them, they would tear up. They would also tear apart on the grill when you tried to turn them. But he had already bought them and wouldn't listen.

The efficiency bit went even further. When cooking all these thin pieces of meat, or whatever it was, we had to take them up quickly lest they dry out too much. We were therefore accustomed to putting them onto trays, using long handled spatulas. They were then taken to a long table where the good wives and mothers who worked the concession stand would put them into buns and wrap them up. Well, the efficiency expert figured that we could save one step by putting the buns on the grill to the left of the meat and then putting the buns onto them with spatulas. This slowed things down considerably since the chef had to line the meat up on the bun before taking it off the spatula. The result was that some of the patties were cooked too long, although, yes, it did eliminate one step in the process.

Well, I simply didn't enjoy cooking hamburgers in this manner and I didn't miss a chance to drop a hint of my displeasure whenever the opportunity arose. I don't recall all the banter, but it became an ongoing bit of oneupsmanship. As the sales of hamburgers fell, the concession lost money because of leftovers. The thing got so bad they reduced the price toward the end of the game, announcing the good deals on the loud speaker. This made it even worse, calling attention to the fact that the hamburgers were not being eaten.

One night, when I knew the efficiency expert was listening, I said that we would sell more burgers and make more money if we put two of those little ol' patties on one bun.

"Look, feller," he said, fed up with me, "This is a ball game. If people want hamburgers, they'll go to Hardee's."

Not me. I'll cook mine at home or in camp, and, of course, one of the best ways to cook a good burger is on a grill. I really don't have a recipe, and I'll sometimes put in such things as parsley and chopped spring onion tops, depending on what I have on hand. I can, however, set forth my basic recipe:

The Basic Burger

For any hamburger, I recommend that you use ground chuck, or ground meat from other relatively low-fat cuts. It is, of course, best if you will buy the meat in chunks, trim the fat, and grind it yourself.

THE MEAT:
1 pound of ground lean meat
½ teaspoon black pepper
salt or seasoning salt
Worcestershire sauce (optional)

GO-WITHS:

mayonnaise	**sliced tomatoes**
steak sauce	**dill or sweet pickles, sliced**
catsup	**fresh, soft buns of regular**
lettuce	**size**
large onion, thinly sliced	**potato chips or french fries**

Build a hot fire in the grill about 30 minutes before you are ready to cook. Mix the pepper into the ground meat and shape it into four patties about ¾ inch thick. You can also mix in ½ teaspoon of salt (or seasoning salt) at this time, or, as I prefer, you can wait and salt each burger when it is almost done. (If you are feeding a mixed group, it's best to have several kinds of seasoning salt at hand, giving them a choice of garlic salt, celery salt, lemon-pepper, smoked salt, and so on. In other words, cook each burger to order.) Grill the meat, uncovered, about 4 inches from the heat, for about 5 minutes on each side. Do not over cook. (If you like Worcestershire sauce, sprinkle a little onto each burger a minute or two before taking off the grill.) The meat should be nicely brown on the outside, but juicy on the inside. If in doubt, cut into a patty before serving it. Of course, each diner will want to fix his or her own burger, with or without onions and other go-withs.

The measures above will make 4 medium-sized burgers. Sometimes, you may want to make larger patties (with half a pound of meat) and use larger buns. It depends on whether you have light eaters or heavy eaters.

Your selection of go-withs might also depend on how you are to serve the hamburgers. On the patio, near the refrigerator, you might easily have a pushcart full of stuff; by campfire, a slice of onion or a few springs of water-cress from a stream will do.

Note on Servings: I like a good chunk of meat in my burgers, and this requires at least ¼ pound of lean meat. With fatty meat, even more may be required because it will shrink during cooking. Usually, two burgers with trimmings will be required to fill me up, but others may get by with one. On a picnic with men, women, and children, allow an average of ⅓ pound of lean meat per person. Have plenty of potato chips or fries.

Suggestion: If you like onion, as I do, you may want to add some to the hamburger meat. If you don't mind the tears, it's best to grate the onion or mince it with a chef's knife. You can also include part of the tops of green onions.

Cheeseburgers

Follow the directions above for The Basic Burger, but vary the toppings and go-withs. I prefer to have sliced ripe tomatoes on cheeseburgers, but not onion. Suit yourself. For the best results, cook one side of the burger as usual. Then turn the meat and put a slice of cheese on top. If you are using a basket, you'll have to unhinge the top part and then add the cheese. Leave the top part of the basket off while cooking the bottom part of the meat.

Italian Burgers

Here's one of my favorites, and I make it with ¼ pound of meat per patty. The measures below make 8 plump, juicy burgers.

2 pounds lean ground meat	**¼ cup olive oil**
2 cups mozzarella cheese, shredded	**2 teaspoons salt**
	1 teaspoon pepper
15 ounces tomato sauce	**1 teaspoon Italian seasoning mix**
1 large onion	
8 ounces fresh mushrooms	**8 hamburger buns**
4 cloves garlic	

Start the fire in the grill. Peel the onion and slice it into ½ inch wheels. In a skillet, heat the olive oil and sauté the onion wheels. When tender, separate the onion into rings and drain on absorbent paper. Mince the garlic and sauté in the remaining oil. (Add a little oil if needed.) Chop the mushrooms and add to the skillet. Sauté for about 10 minutes. Stir in the tomato sauce and Italian seasoning mix, along with ½ teaspoon of the salt and ¼ teaspoon of the pepper. Simmer for a while, then remove from the heat.

Mix the meat, 1½ teaspoons salt, and ¾ teaspoon pepper. Divide the meat into 16 equal parts. Shape into thin patties. Put ¼ cup of cheese on each of the 8 patties, then top each one with the remaining patties. Close the edges with your fingers. Then put the patties into a hinged basket and cook over medium hot coals for 6 to 8 minutes on each side, or until done.

Spread some of the sauce on the bottom half of each bun, then top with a meat patty. Next, add some sautéed onion rings on each meat patty, then spread on some sauce. Note that the onion rings can be omitted from some of the burgers.

Hamburger Steak

My family is fond of grilled hamburger steaks, which I make with the aid of a hinged grilling basket. I use only ground round, ground chuck, or similar low-fat meat.

2½ to 3 pounds lean ground beef
minced garlic or grated onion, or both
salt
freshly ground black pepper
Worcestershire sauce

Build a good charcoal fire and adjust the rack a good ways from the heat—7 or 8 inches. Mix the minced garlic (or onion, or both), salt, and pepper into the meat. Shape the meat into a steak about an 1 ¼ inches thick, then carefully put the steak into the basket. Close the basket and lock it shut. Put the steak over the coals and cook for 10 minutes on each side. (The exact timing depends on how thick the meat is, how far your rack is from the coals, etc.) Without unhinging the basket, I test the steak with a fork. I like it when the inside is still a little pink. Others will want it well done. (Remember, however, that this steak will not be served up with gravy; if you want it to be moist and succulent, do not overcook it.) When the steak is almost ready to take up, I squirt on a little Worcestershire sauce. Cut the steak into pieces and serve it with baked potatoes, tossed salad, and bread. I allow from ½ to ¾ pound of meat per person.

Variation: This same recipe can be used for direct cooking in a covered grill. Add a few good wood chips if you want some smoke.

Grilled Meat Balls

Although the Turkish *shish kabob* is popular in the Middle East and in other parts of the world, the Arabs as well as the Iranians have another interesting way of grilling meat. Instead of stringing up chunks of lamb or camel or other good meat on a skewer, they shape ground meat around a skewer and grill it over hot coals. Usually, this skewer has a flat, sword-shaped blade, so that the meat stays on it better. Also, both ends of the skewer rest across the coals, with no support in the middle. In other words, no grid is used. To accomplish this at home, I use two bricks with the coals between them, and a third brick is used in the rear. The trouble with a rack, of course, is that the meat tends to stick to it and tear off the skewer.

The Arabs prefer a finely ground meat. More often than not, lamb is specified, but I normally cook the dish with beef or a combination of beef and pork, which I run through the grinder twice. I suspect that any combination of good meat can be used, such as turtle and camel. Personally, I am fond of the method for cooking what I consider to be inferior cuts. In other words, I use the tenderloin for *shish kabob,* and the recipe below for the tougher cuts. I also like the method because it allows one to mix the spices into the meat rather than swabbing them onto the surface.

2 pounds of finely ground meat	**½ teaspoon dried thyme**
I chicken egg	**½ teaspoon ground coriander**
2 medium onions, chopped	**½ teaspoon ground cumin**
I tablespoon chopped fresh parsley, or ½ tablespoon dried parsley	**I teaspoon salt**
	⅛ teaspoon cayenne pepper

Mix all the ingredients well and set the mixture in the refrigerator for an hour or longer. Build a fire and rig for grilling. When the coals are ready, shape the meat mixture around a skewer into balls, about 1½ inches in diameter. Fill up the skewer, but don't pack the balls together. Put the skewers across the coals and grill until done, turning frequently. I prefer mine to be cooked for 10 minutes about 4 inches from hot coals, but cooking times will vary, depending on your fire and your rig. In any case, the inside of the balls should be done but quite moist.

I serve the meat over a bed of rice.

Variations: The spices in this dish can be varied to suit your taste or your meat, or both. Camel, for example, or even mutton, might benefit from a bit more cumin. Or you can omit all of the spices, except perhaps the salt and cayenne pepper. (Black pepper can be used instead of the cayenne pepper.)

The Arabs cook a similar dish by shaping the ground meat onto the skewer in a long sausage shape instead of in balls. Suit yourself. In Iran, my wife informs me, they use sword-shaped skewers and shape the ground meat around it, then they pull it off with the aid of a flat, pliable bread, not unlike the Mexican tortilla. Sometimes they eat the meat in the bread, and sometimes they eat it separately.

Grilled Kibbeh

When I worked with the Lew Childre & Son's fishing tackle firm some years ago, a burly fellow by the name of Shag Shahid made *kibbeh* from time to time and we ate it raw. He was very, very careful about where he bought the meat and how it had been handled. I understand that he used lean beef, and that he ground it several times before mixing in the other ingredients. I don't know exactly what he had in the mixture, but it was very good. Lew said that while eating Shag's *kibbeh* he could feel his strength gathering.

Kibbeh, of course, is a favorite dish in Syria and Lebanon, where it is eaten raw as well as cooked. It is usually eaten on a leaf of lettuce, along with a drop or two of juice squeezed from a lemon. Being good ol' boys, most of us at Lew's ate the stuff atop saltines, as if it were potted meat or sardines. I still like it that way. The tenderfoots among us usually required lots of saltines, and maybe more than a drop or two of Worcestershire sauce.

But I really can't recommend, in a book like this, that anyone eat raw meat these days. Fortunately, *kibbeh* can also be cooked in a number of ways, and grilling over hot coals is a favorite. I highly recommend that you try it. Here's what you'll need:

> **2 pounds lean lamb or beef, finely ground**
> **2 medium-to-large onions, grated**
> **3 cups fine cracked wheat** (bulgur)
> **salt and pepper to taste**
> **olive oil** (optional)

Grind the meat several times. In Syria, both the meat and cracked wheat are pounded by hand in a stone mortar with a pestle. (A modern practitioner in another country finds it easier to use a food processor, or to run it through a food grinder with a fine blade three times.) In any case, make sure that the meat is finely ground, but not soupy. Rinse the cracked wheat in a sieve and press it to force the water out. Mix the meat and onion (the onion should also be finely grated; it can also be ground) thoroughly, grinding and pounding it in a mortar or with an electric mixer. Salt and pepper to taste. Mix in the cracked wheat, grinding and pounding again in the mortar or in a mixer, adding a little water from time to time with a spoon. The idea behind all this grinding is to get a smooth texture.

Build a charcoal fire in your grill (or heat up a gas or electric unit). Shape the *kibbeh* into patties about ¾ inch thick and 3 inches wide. Place the patties about 4 inches above the hot coals and grill until done, 6 to 8 minutes on each side, or until the surface is golden. If you have very lean meat, you may want to brush the patties lightly with olive oil while grilling.

Grilled Hobo

I've never been too fond of wrapping meat in aluminum foil before grilling it over a charcoal fire. Such meat doesn't get any of the smoke from the fire, or the direct heat, either, and it is more steamed than grilled. Nonetheless, aluminum foil comes in handy for cooking such dishes as the hobo. I see this one as a dish for cooking in camp or at a roadside park instead of on the patio. The ingredients below will make a complete meal for one. If you've got more folks to feed, simply make each one a separate hobo.

> ¼ **pound lean ground beef**
> I **potato, sliced into ¼-inch wheels**
> I **carrot, sliced into ¼ inch wheels**
> I **onion, sliced ¼ inch thick**
> **garlic salt**
> **salt**
> **black pepper**

Sprinkle the meat with a little garlic salt and black pepper. Shape it into a patty the size of a normal hamburger. Place the meat patty on a square of heavy-duty aluminum foil. Top with potato slices, sliced carrots, and onion rings. Sprinkle with salt and black pepper. Carefully fold the aluminum foil, sealing all edges. Put the hobo onto a hot grill for 15 minutes. Unwrap the hobo carefully, in case you have to put it back together. (If you are cooking more than one, as will usually be the case, leave the rest on the grill while you test one.) The meat should be browned and the vegetables should be done. Be sure to test the carrots with a fork. If they are soft, you're ready to eat, provided that the meat patty was not too thick.

If you want to live dangerously, try cooking the hobo directly atop a few hot coals raked out of a campfire. It's best to wrap the meat and vegetables twice with heavy-duty aluminum foil, making two separate wraps. For success, it is important that the foil be closed tightly so that it will hold in the juices and steam. If you have doubts about using this method in camp, test it at home in the fireplace.

GRILLING KABOBS

During the TV newscasts of Operation Desert Shield, any outdoor chef worth his seasoning salt took note of the street vendors of Baghdad cooking kabobs in a small trough-like grill or firebox. The skewers were only about 8 inches long, and they fitted across the grill in equidistant slots, thereby requiring no grid. While grilling the meat, the street vendor kept a hand-held fan in constant motion to keep a hot fire going. I've never used such a box, but I do often rig for grilling kabobs between bricks. No grid is needed because the kabob skewers reach from one side to the other, and such a set can be made in camp, in the fireplace, or even in a large grill with the racks removed. My favorite skewer for this kind of cooking is made of thin, flat metal. The ones that I own have a wooden handle. They came from Iran, although similar designs are available elsewhere. In any case, the flat design keeps the kabobs from rolling and the wooden handle makes them easy to pick up or turn. I always take the meat off the skewer, however, before serving it. If you want to serve the meat on the stick, you might try those disposable wooden skewers or something a little fancy, such as polished metal skewers shaped like a long dagger.

Frankly, I prefer to have my vegetables cooked separately instead of strung up between the meat. For one thing, the meat and the several kinds of vegetables should, ideally, have different cooking times. But I'll allow that bell peppers and onions can add a good flavor to the meat if everything is jammed up pretty tight. Further, the vegetables make an attractive kabob, if everything works right. Too often, I say, the outside edges of the bell pepper will be burned and the inside will be raw. I suspect that some restaurants that serve up perfect looking kabobs, on a bed of rice, cook the meat and vegetables separately, then string everything up on a skewer, then lay the thing across a bed of rice. From the economic point of view, an advantage of such a kabob is that it won't hold much meat. Me, I would prefer to have the skewer full of meat with the vegetables around the rim of the rice bed. But, suit yourself. Some of the recipes below call for vegetables, but most don't. Add them if you like. Also remember that mushrooms go exceptionally well with kabobs, partly because most of the button-shaped mushrooms available in a market are a convenient size and partly because the button mushroom is one vegetable that is good whether it is cooked for a long time or a short time.

Shish Kabob

This famous Turkish dish, *sis kabob,* now enjoyed the world over, is said to have been developed and spread by the conquering soldiers of the Ottoman Empire. Supposedly they strung up cubes of freshly killed lamb (or mutton) onto their swords and grilled them over hot coals. (Meat cooked on a sword is also called *kars kabob.*) The fresh lamb meat, it was discovered, is improved by a simple marinade, as set forth in the recipe below.

> **tender lamb, cut into cubes**
> **olive oil**
> **lemon juice**
> **sliced onion**
> **salt and pepper**

Trim the lamb and cut it into cubes. Mix a marinade of olive oil, lemon juice, and sliced onion. Put the meat into a nonmetallic container and pour the marinade over it. Marinate for 1 hour or longer. Put the lamb on skewers and grill it over hot coals until the meat is browned on the outside—but juicy and pink on the inside. To achieve this balance, put the meat within 3 or 4 inches of hot coals, cook for 7 or 8 minutes, then turn and cook the other side for 6 or 7 minutes, or until done. Salt and pepper to taste while kabobs are still very hot. Cooking meat quickly over hot coals requires constant attention, and drying the meat out makes it tough and chewy. The meat may also be basted with the leftover marinade, which will help keep it succulent.

In Turkey, *shish kabob* is often served with rice and sliced tomatoes. The combination is hard to beat. I don't offer exact measures for the marinade, but I usually use about ½ cup olive oil, juice of I lemon, and I medium sliced onion to marinate enough lamb to feed my family of four.

Variations: There are infinite variations on the marinade throughout the Middle East and the rest of the world. My wife says that her friends from Armenia use the exact marinade, but that they add lots of flaked red pepper to it. I'm all for that, too. In Turkey, Greece, and other countries, slices or quarters of onions, tomatoes, and bell peppers are put onto the skewers between the pieces of meat. But remember that the recipe set forth above is a classic, and that cookbook and magazine writers seem to have a need to add stuff to simple dishes. Do so at your culinary peril.

Kabobs of the Caucasus

Many people believe that the kabob originated in Russia or in the Caucasus, where they are highly popular even today. The kabobs of this area are made from several meats, including lamb, kid goat, fish, beef, pork, venison, and bear. Usually, the meat is marinated in onion juice, wine vinegar, or pomegranate juice, then skewered and grilled over charcoal. Often, the lamb is alternated on the skewer with pieces of onion. In some areas, especially Azerbaijan, the meat is alternated with chunks of fat obtained from under the tail of a special kind of sheep that is bred in the area. The kabobs are usually eaten with vegetables or over a platter of rice. They are also eaten with a sauce made of pomegranate or sour plums.

Indonesian Kabobs

The food from Indonesia is quite varied, as one would expect from what Marco Polo called the "Spice Islands." In addition to local ingredients, such as a dark sugar made from the sap of coconut or palmyra palm trees, the islanders have made good use of other foods, such as hot peppers and peanuts from the Americas. Almost all Indonesian meals are served with white rice. If you grill the kabobs in the recipe below, consider using bamboo skewers and, when the meat is ready, serve the kabobs atop a bed of rice. I serve mine right on the skewers.

Remember that the sauce can be cooked in the kitchen before you start grilling the meat. The meat is discussed first, however, because it must be marinated for several hours.

THE MEAT:
1 pound of tender beef
1 pound of lean pork
¼ cup dark brown sugar
2 tablespoons soy sauce
1 tablespoon rice vinegar
1 tablespoon ground coriander seed
1 clove garlic, minced

Trim the meats, cut it into 1-inch cubes, and put them into a nonmetallic container. Mix the brown sugar, soy sauce, vinegar, coriander, and garlic. Pour the mixture over the meats and toss to coat all sides. Marinate the meat for several hours. When you are ready to cook, build a charcoal fire or heat up the gas or electric grill. Put the meat onto the skewers, fixing a separate skewer for each guest. Alternate pork and beef, or give your guests their choice. Grill about 4 inches from the heat for 6 or 7 minutes. Turn and cook for another 6 or 7 minutes. Do not cook too long, but make sure that the pork is done. (Remember that the thickness of the meat has a lot to do with cooking times. It is not a bad idea to cut the pork a little thinner than the beef, just to make sure it is done while leaving the beef medium rare.)

Serve the kabobs with rice, giving each guest both beef and pork—or their choice. It's best to divide the servings before putting the meat onto the skewers; then you serve the meat by putting the skewers onto a bed of rice, or by stripping the meat off the skewer onto a bed of rice. In any case, top each serving of meat with sauce, made as directed below.

THE SAUCE:

¼ cup crunchy peanut butter

¼ cup butter, margarine, or oil

2 tablespoons dark brown sugar

juice of 1 lemon

1 medium onion, minced

2 cloves garlic, minced

2 tablespoons water

1 tablespoon rice vinegar

1 teaspoon red pepper flakes

Heat the water in a small pan and add the red pepper flakes to it. While the pepper is steeping, heat the butter (or margarine or oil) and sauté the onion and garlic. Add the pepper flakes (and the liquid from the pan), lemon juice, vinegar, brown sugar, and peanut butter. Heat and stir, but do not boil. Remove from the heat, but keep warm until the kabobs are ready to eat.

Servings: I allow about ½ pound of meat per person if I am feeding heavy eaters. But ⅓ of a pound will do, and the above measures will feed from 4 to 6. You can add (or subtract) a pound or so of meat without having to adjust the measures for the sauce or marinade.

Note: A similar dish is also very popular in Malaysia. It too is served over rice and with a peanut sauce.

Oyster Kabobs

Oysters are frequently wrapped in bacon, pinned with a toothpick, and broiled in the oven. The are even better when cooked on the grill, kabob-style, with mushrooms. Here's my recipe:

medium oysters, freshly shucked	½ cup margarine
fresh mushrooms	juice of 2 lemons
2 tablespoons minced parsley	⅛ teaspoon cayenne pepper
cornstarch	sweet Hungarian paprika
	bacon, ½ strip per oyster

Build a fire in your grill. While the coals are getting hot, melt the margarine in a saucepan. Stir in the lemon juice, cayenne pepper, and I tablespoon of the minced parsley. (Save the rest of the parsley.) Keep the sauce warm. In a skillet, fry the bacon until it is opaque but still limp. (Note: You'll need ½ strip of bacon for each oyster, and have enough mushroom caps to alternate with the oysters.) Remove the bacon and sauté the mushrooms in the bacon drippings for a few minutes. Drain.

When the coals are ready, cut the bacon strips in half. Sprinkle each bacon half lightly with minced parsley. Drain the oysters and dust them with cornstarch. Wrap each oyster with half a bacon strip, rolling so that the parsley is inside. Thread the wrapped oysters onto skewers, alternating with whole mushroom caps. Brush each kabob with lemon sauce and place it over the hot coals. (I like mine about 4 inches from the coals.) Cook for 5 minutes, or until the bacon browns, turn, and cook for 5 minutes on the other side. The bacon may drip badly, so watch out for fires. I prefer to cook this dish on a large grill so that I can move the kabobs from one spot to another if fires do occur. Before serving, brush the kabobs with lemon sauce and sprinkle generously with paprika.

Although I could make a meal of this dish, especially with a little rice and a vegetable or two, it goes best as an appetizer. Remember that it cooks rather quickly and can be taken off the grill before the coals are burned down too low. In other words, serve the oysters as appetizers while you finish grilling red meat or other fare for the main feed.

Game Kabobs

At home or in camp, one of my very favorite ways to prepare very tender venison is to wrap little squares of meat in bacon and cook them on a stick or skewer over hot coals. Usually, I use the tenderloin for this purpose, especially in camp.

Cut the pieces into cubes of 1½ inches. Salt and pepper each piece, wrap it with half a strip of thin-sliced bacon, and stick it onto a skewer blade. Fill the skewer and put it over hot coals. (I like for mine to be about four inches from the heat.) Cook the kabobs until the bacon is done but not quite crisp on one side. Turn and cook the other side the same way. Then sprinkle both sides lightly with paprika and cook a little more, until the bacon is crisp on top and bottom. (If you use thick sliced bacon, partly cook it in a skillet before wrapping the venison with it.)

Be warned that cooking anything wrapped in bacon over hot coals is a full time job. Grease fires caused by bacon drippings can easily burn your meat while you are talking on the telephone. I like to have a wide area of coals, so that I can simply move a skewer of meat over in case the bacon drips too much and starts a fire. Other people use water in a squirt bottle to control the flame.

Serve the venison kabobs on a bed of rice, along with your choice of bread and vegetables. I prefer French bread and San Francisco frozen vegetables, stir fried.

Note: Unless you have very tender meat, it's best to marinate it or use some commercial tenderizer before making kabobs. If in doubt, soak the venison in buttermilk for several hours before cooking it. Powdered buttermilk, when properly mixed with water, will do in camp.

Shark Kabobs

The Chinese and other Orientals have a way with shark, and the marinade used in this recipe is heavily influenced by them. Be sure to try it. Any shark that is sold in fish markets should be suitable. If you catch your own, however, remember that the fish ought to be gutted or bled and put on ice immediately. If you are out at sea and have to head back to the dock to hoist your catch up for pictures, chances are that the meat will not be as good. The larger the shark, the more important it becomes to gut and ice the fish as soon as possible. Remember also that some fresh shark meat contains ammonia and smells accordingly. This smell can be eliminated by cutting the meat into fillets, steaks, or chunks and soaking it in salt water for a few minutes. Then proceed with the following.

THE MEAT AND MARINADE
2 pounds shark meat, cubed into 1½-inch chunks
½ cup rice wine or sherry
½ cup soy sauce
¼ cup peanut oil
juice of 1 lemon
2 cloves garlic, minced
½ teaspoon freshly ground ginger

VEGETABLES
cherry tomatoes
onions, about the size of cherry tomatoes
button mushrooms of suitable size
bell pepper, cut into 1½-inch pieces

Mix the marinade ingredients. Marinate the meat in a glass container for 2 hours under refrigeration. Build a charcoal fire. Arrange the shark chunks on skewers, along with tomatoes, onions, mushrooms, and bell pepper. Put the skewers about 6 inches from the hot coals. Turn and baste with remaining marinade several times while cooking for 10 to 15 minutes, or until the meat flakes easily when tested with a fork. Serve over rice.

Variations: This recipe can be used with other fish that have a texture suitable for cooking on a skewer. Try it with swordfish.

94

Moroccan Kabobs

Kabobs are popular all over the Arab world, although they might be called brochettes in regions that have been heavily influenced by the French. Of course, lamb is a popular meat for kabobs, but beef, hump of camel, pork loin, and other good meats can be used. In most kabobs, a marinade is a required part of the recipe. After cooking, the meat is topped with a sauce, as in the recipe below.

2 or 3 pounds lamb
¼ cup olive oil
¼ cup vinegar
1 large onion, grated
1 tablespoon of minced fresh parsley

1 tablespoon paprika
1 teaspoon cumin or finely ground cumin seeds
1 teaspoon salt
1 teaspoon black pepper

Wash the lamb, cut it into kabob-size pieces, and put them into a nonmetallic bowl. Mix the other ingredients and pour over the lamb. Toss to coat all sides of the meat. Refrigerate overnight, or at least 8 hours, stirring once or twice. If you prefer, use a large Ziploc bag in which to marinate the meat.

Build a charcoal fire. While the coals are burning down, prepare a sauce as follows:

1 small can tomato paste (6 ounces)
1 tomato paste can of vinegar (6 ounces)
½ tomato paste can of olive oil
1 teaspoon salt
Tabasco or Louisiana hot sauce to taste

Mix the ingredients in a saucepan and warm. (The Moroccans prefer the tomato sauce to be quite hot, but suit yourself.) Thin it a little with water. Keep it warm while you cook the meat.

Put the meat onto skewers and cook over hot coals for 5 or 6 minutes on each side, or until done to your satisfaction. Remove the meat from the skewers and serve it with the sauce. Have plenty of hot French bread at hand.

GRILLING SAUSAGES AND VARIETY MEATS

Well, I'll be honest about it. This heading came about at the last minute in order to catch a few entries that don't fit neatly elsewhere. For example, something ought to be said, in a book like this, about sausages and the great American hotdog. Although I prefer beef wieners, these days it's hard to tell what a hotdog has got in it, and putting the hotdog under the heading of beef would be highly misleading. Even chicken is used in hotdogs these days. Even so, you ask, why put "hotdog" under "variety meats," which include tripe, tongue, heart, testicles, and so on. I'll tell you that even beef wieners don't contain much T-bone steak.

Before dropping this subject, I would like to add that variety meats, such as sweetbreads and sheep "fries" can be grilled successfully, and anyone who likes them, as I do, won't hesitate to put them onto a grill, along with other meats. Experiment and enjoy—but don't force this sort of thing on your guests. In fact, it's best not to discuss such topics while eating. Even if you bring it up in a group of daring gourmets, someone is going to have recipe for sheep gut, cleaned and wrapped around a stick and grilled to perfection, with a touch of salt, as commonly cooked on the deserts of North Africa. I'll also add that all of us have personal limits, which will vary from one to another. One sport might not blink at chittlings, but would turn away from the table if a fish eyeball were served. With some people, tongue might do the trick. Or moose nose. With me, it's blood sausage. I don't want any, grilled or otherwise, if I know what it is. In any case, I don't consider most of the variety meats, except for liver, to be especially suited for the grill. Some parts, such as the brain, are too soft to be handled. Others, such as the heart, are too tough—yet grilled beef heart is a specialty in Australia, and can be successful, if it's not cooked very long, as indicated in the recipe below.

96

Grilled Beef Hearts

An animal heart is really nothing but a muscle. Since it works continuously, it tends to be tough and is usually more suited to long, slow, cooking. But it can also be grilled, and is quite popular in Australia. Here's my method:

beef heart
butter
lemon juice
salt and pepper to taste

Slice the beef heart into ½ inch wheels. Squeeze a little lemon juice on each piece and let set until the coals are hot in the grill. Brush the pieces with melted butter, then salt and pepper to taste. Grill very close to the coals for 3 minutes on each side. If you overcook this cut of meat, it will be as tough as the sole of a shoe.

Since this dish cooks so quickly, you might try it as an appetizer for you and your guests to eat while waiting on the thick-cut steaks to cook. After cooking, you may want to dice the meat into small pieces and serve with toothpicks and lemon-butter sauce.

Liver

Although I specify calf's liver for this recipe, I am fond of grilling other kinds of liver—especially fresh venison liver. Even chicken liver can be cooked on a grill if a hinged basket is used to facilitate turning.

I pound calf liver, ½ inch thick
¼ cup olive oil
¼ cup onion juice (see below)
salt and pepper

Build a good fire. Squeeze some onion juice by using a garlic press or by first zapping an onion in a food processor and then pushing it through a sieve. Mix the onion juice and olive oil, then rub some onto both sides of the liver. When the coals burn down, grill the liver for about 4 minutes close to the heat. Baste lightly with oil and onion juice. Do not overcook. The grilled liver should be pink on the inside. Salt and pepper each piece to taste, then serve.

In camp, try this recipe with fresh venison liver cooked over a wood fire. If you don't have a grid, cut the liver into strips and hang them over a stick. Use bacon grease instead of olive oil, and omit the onion juice if necessary.

Grilled Hotdogs

A wiener roast is always fun around a campfire or hearth. The patio grill can also be used to advantage, and, when cooking hamburgers for a mixed group, I'll often put on wieners or frankfurters for those who prefer hotdogs. They are very easy to grill. I place mine here and there, often among other kinds of meat, and grill them for 4 or 5 minutes. Then I turn them and grill the other side. (I also like to cook wieners along with meat that is to be flavored with smoke, usually under a covered hood.) Grilled wieners are usually served on hotdog buns, along with the usual mustard, catsup, and so on. I like lots of chopped onions on mine.

Note: Chili is a great addition to hotdogs made with wieners that have been boiled or steamed, but it tends to distract from the flavor of grilled wieners, especially if it is highly seasoned.

Link Sausage

It's hard to go wrong with good seasoned sausage. There must be a hundred kinds, with thousands of variations, made of pork, beef, lamb, and other meats. I usually buy a smoked beef sausage. Pork sausage tends to be very fatty, which can cause some problems on a grill. Usually, however, you can find a local sausage maker who will make you a batch with ham and the leaner cuts of pork. Good stuff.

With most sausage, already highly seasoned and smoked, all you have to do is put them on the grill and cook until the sides are nicely browned. I usually prick the skin here and there with a fork to allow some of the fat to escape.

Normally, I grill sausage as an extra meat, to be used in case you need it to feed everybody. In some areas, grilled sausage is commonly available at a cook-out type barbecue. In South Africa, for example, the large *boerewors* (boer sausage) are traditionally served at a *braai,* or cookout, along with grilled lamb.

Sweetbreads

Forget all about first poaching sweetbreads in water and lemon juice and other stuff and then carefully removing the membrane. If you like sweet-breads—and I do—then simply cut them in half, sprinkle lightly with lemon juice, and grill them quite close to hot coals for 3 or 4 minutes. During the last minute or so of cooking, sprinkle them lightly with salt and pepper.

GRILLING FRUITS AND VEGETABLES

These days we seem to be eating more and more vegetables with less and less meat. Some vegetables can be cooked quite successfully on the grill, and some, such as fresh corn, are terrific fare and have become more or less traditional at some cookouts.

One problem is that cooking vegetables along with the meat takes up space on the grill. Consequently, a large grid is highly desirable for modern family cooking. For a family of four or six, a grill with a hinged cover is recommended.

Onion Slices

If you've got large, mild onions try cutting them into ¾-inch slices and grilling them over hot coals. I usually slice the onion without peeling it, then stick a couple of toothpicks into the slice to help hold the rings together. After grilling, I remove the toothpicks and peel off the outer ring. Here's what you'll need:

> **large onions**
> **melted butter or margarine (for basting)**
> **heavy whipping cream**
> **garlic salt**
> **freshly ground black pepper**

Slice the onions. Sprinkle one side with garlic salt and freshly ground black pepper. Turn the slices over and coat the face-up sides with heavy whipping cream, then sprinkle with garlic salt and pepper. Put the onion slices into a wire rack and close it. Build a tent with aluminum foil and cover the rack. Grill for 10 minutes with the cream side up, basting with butter (or margarine) after 5 minutes. Turn the grill, baste with butter (or margarine), and grill the cream sides for 5 to 10 minutes, or until the onions are starting to brown.

Serve the grilled onion slices with any meat. They are especially fitting with grilled liver.

Mushrooms

There are so many kinds of wild mushrooms that a blanket recipe or statement simply cannot be made. The most common form of cultivated mushrooms, white and rounded, or button-shaped, are excellent for the grill. For one reason, they contain lots of moisture, and can therefore be cooked for a long time or a short time. In other words, it's hard to go wrong with these. Long grilling makes the white mushroom look worse—but improves the flavor.

Unless I am making kabobs, I normally leave the stem on these mushrooms. The larger ones can be cut in half, or sliced. Grill with or without marinade, with or without olive oil or butter.

Turnip Roots

Choose fresh, almost mature turnip roots of medium to large size. Slice them into ½-inch wheels. Grill over medium or hot coals for 10 minutes on each side, basting from time to time with oil or melted butter. Season lightly with salt and pepper before serving.

Smaller, younger roots (about the size of a golf ball) can be peeled and grilled whole, or halved.

If you like grilled turnip roots, also try grilled rutabaga slices.

Potatoes

One of my favorite recipes for potatoes was set forth in the recipe on page 50. To recap, slice the potatoes into ½ inch wheels, coat with zesty Italian salad dressing, and grill for a total of about 10 minutes on each side, turning once. If you don't care for the zesty touch, remember that the sliced potatoes can also be coated with oil, and sprinkled with garlic salt or some other seasoning. I also like them basted with melted butter and sprinkled lightly with paprika and a touch of salt.

Small new potatoes can be cooked whole on the grill, and will usually require about 30 minutes. Larger potatoes must be cooked for a longer period of time, usually under a covered grill. Some people wrap them in aluminum foil.

Sweet Potatoes and Yams

These are different vegetables, but both can be grilled to advantage. After washing, cut them lengthwise into slices about ½-inch thick. Rub with melted butter or oil, and grill for 10 minutes on each side. Brush with butter, then sprinkle on some brown sugar. Grill for a few minutes on each side. Serve while hot.

Sweet potatoes can also be baked in a covered grill. If you are building a campfire to cook on, try burying a few sweet potatoes an inch or two under the ground; then build the fire over them. You can also bury them in hot ashes in camp or on the hearth at home. The thick skin may char in spots, but this doesn't hurt a thing. The sweet potato is one vegetable that benefits from long, slow cooking, up to a point.

Squash and Zucchini

Yes, squash of all sorts can be grilled. Even zucchini. Usually, it is best to select rather small squash or zucchini, cut them in half lengthwise, then grill for 10 minutes on each side, or until tender. Lightly baste once or twice with melted butter or oil.

Larger gooseneck squash, as well as those of squat shape, can be sliced into wheels instead of being merely split. Tiny squash can be cooked whole. The chayote and button-shaped squash can be cut in half, making two wheels, and grilled without peeling. Eat these with a spoon, scooping the meat off the peeling, as when eating a cold melon with the rind still on it.

Corn

Fresh corn—the fresher the better—is one of the truly choice vegetables to grill. You want "roasting ears," with the kernels plump and very juicy but not hard. For best results, pull your corn off the stalk and put it onto the grill immediately. Grill it for 20 minutes, turning from time to time. Peel back the shucks and pick out the silk strands. Good as is, or you can brush on a little melted butter and salt.

That's the way I do it. Anyone who can't shuck and pick the silk from the corn doesn't deserve to eat it. But there are other opinions, and most experts at the grill recommend that you first pull back the shucks, pick off the silks, and put the shucks back together again before grilling the ear. Some experts recommend that the ears be soaked in water for half an hour before putting them onto the grill. But I don't think this is necessary, if you've got really fresh ears. Also, you can always use your basting brush to apply a little water if the corn shucks seem in danger of browning too much.

My wife tells me that in Iran, corn is grilled in this manner. When it is almost done, however, the ears are dipped into salted water, then put back onto the grill for a few minutes before eating. It's delicious that way.

I don't recommend that frozen corn be grilled, but sometimes ears are partly shucked, picked, trimmed, packed in boxes, and covered with plastic film wrap for display in supermarkets. Most of these don't have enough shuck left on them to protect the kernels from browning or to provide moisture. I sometimes grill these after first soaking them for a few minutes in water and then wrapping them tightly in aluminum foil.

Note: If you've got access to a good field of green corn and a stream full of trout or smallmouth bass, try grilling fish inside shucks. It's best to pull back the shucks, then cut out the ear of corn, leaving the shucks intact. Put the fish inside the cavity; add a little butter, salt, and pepper. Tie off the end of the shucks on the silk end with a string or a twist wire. Grill on both sides for 10 minutes or so, depending on how thick the fish are. Test one before serving. When done, the fish will flake easily with a fork. The corn shucks impart a flavor that is unique and haunting. General Wade Hampton, a bear hunter, is said to have enjoyed fish cooked by a variation of this method. He put a small strip of bacon, butter, salt, and pepper inside the fish, then wrapped it with shucks and put the whole works into the hot coals. The ears of corn were roasted before the fire, perhaps stuck onto the end of sharpened sticks.

Tomatoes

Summer is a happy time for gardeners and chefs, for that's when the best vine-ripened tomatoes are readily available. These can be grilled, but, frankly, they are better when merely sliced and served with barbecued or grilled meat. Green tomatoes are another matter, and I always grill a few when I can't wait for them to ripen. Select large tomatoes that are almost mature but have not yet turned red. Slice these into ¾-inch rounds and grill them for 5 or 6 minutes on each side, or until tender. Salt lightly after grilling. The Mexican husk tomatoes, *tomatillos,* can be cooked in the same way, although they aren't as large as regular tomatoes.

For kabobs, cherry tomatoes can be used whole or cut in half.

Pineapple

The flavor of pineapple goes nicely with cured ham that has been grilled, and I prefer to use quartered unpeeled pineapples, prepared and cooked as described in the recipe on page 51. But I do sometimes peel, core, and slice pineapples for the grill. Even canned wheels of pineapple can be grilled to advantage. Just put them atop the grid until they start to brown, then turn and lightly brown the other side.

Carrots

Select carrots of medium size. Wash but do not peel. Rub with oil and grill over medium-hot coals for half an hour, or until fairly tender to the fork. Carrots can also be wrapped in foil and cooked for a longer time, giving pretty much the same texture as steamed carrots. By direct grilling, however, you get a carrot that is rather crisp on the outside and soft on the inside. Try them.

Eggplant

Slice ordinary oblong purple eggplant lengthwise into slabs ½-inch thick. Spread these out on a clean towel or absorbent paper. Sprinkle with salt and leave for half an hour. When you are ready to cook, wipe the slices to remove the excess moisture. Baste both sides very lightly with oil, then grill for 7 or 8 minutes on each side. Do not baste while cooking. The eggplant will become soggy and greasy if it is basted often or heavily.

The smaller Japanese eggplants can be cut in half lengthwise, and grilled on both sides until tender.

Bananas and Plantains

In some parts of the world, green plantains are frequently used in cooking. These can be cut in half and grilled to advantage. You can also use underripe bananas, which will be slightly green in color, whenever you can find them in your local markets. Cut these in half and grill them, skin up, for a few minutes. Then turn them skin down and brush the meat with melted butter and sprinkle with brown sugar. Grill until the fruit is tender and the skin begins to brown overly.

I like to grill whole bananas and top them with a sauce made by melting 2 tablespoons of butter, and then stirring in 2 tablespoons lemon juice, two tablespoons brown sugar, and ½ teaspoon of ground allspice. When the bananas have finished grilling, slice them in half lengthwise. Spoon some of the warm sauce over each banana half. I usually serve the grilled bananas in the peel, and eat them with a spoon.

Apples and Pears

Select firm, rather tart apples. Core the apples but do not peel them. Cut them into slices and grill until they start to brown and are tender to the fork. Baste lightly with butter. Pears can be grilled the same way. Both pears and apples can be cored and grilled in halves.

Part Three

INDIRECT COOKING

The equipment and techniques set forth in this section are ideally suited for cooking large chunks of meat in some sort of patio or outdoor rig, although the techniques can also be used for chicken and other smaller pieces. The indirect method is also used in connection with the terms "smoking" and "barbecuing," which to me are really means of flavoring meat instead of methods of cooking it. The purist might argue that "barbecue" is a method of cooking, but a quick glance at recipes in modern cookbooks will reveal barbecue recipes for cooking in the kitchen oven, in a skillet, under a broiler, atop a grid, and in a hole in the ground. Smoking and barbecuing are discussed at length in the Parts Four and Five.

COVERED WAGON GRILLS

While eating one night at Choctawhatchee Lodge, where I sometimes cook a dish or two for deer hunters, a big fellow hunched over his bowl of venison-bone soup while I expounded on the recipe for making it. Although he gulped my soup down with gusto, I knew that he really wasn't interested in soups or crock-pot recipes. I had, in fact, already pegged him as a jackleg patio chef, and I wasn't surprised when he broke into one of my sentences to ask me how I cooked a whole ham from a deer. I went on with the particulars of the venison-bone soup recipe, pretending not to hear him. He asked again, loud enough now to stop all other chatter at the table.

"Cook it slowly," I advised, "in a huge, tightly covered cast-iron Dutch oven."

"I mean how do you cook it on a *grill?*" the guy said, looking straight at me. Everybody quit eating to hear my answer.

"Look," I said, "it would be better to separate the ham, as you call it, into sections and cook them as small roasts—or cut them into chops."

"Not necessarily," said an international sport by the name of Walter Allen of Montgomery, Alabama. A quiet, neat type, he touched up the corners of his mouth with a white napkin and then proceeded to set forth his recipe and method for cooking a "ham" from the fallow deer that he stalks on a castle estate somewhere in Ireland.

Later, I tried Allen's recipe on an ordinary American whitetail, with quite favorable results, and I would like to pass it on. Remember, however, that the success of any recipe for large chunks of venison, fallow or otherwise, depends on having prime meat that has been cleanly killed, quickly dressed, cooled, and properly aged. Here's the recipe:

109

Walter Allen's Hindquarter of Venison

1 hindquarter of deer	12 ounces fresh or canned
4 strips bacon	mushrooms
2 bottles of Italian dressing	4 carrots, diced
(16-ounce size)	4 potatoes, diced
2 cups dry white wine	2 cloves garlic, peeled
1 large onion, sliced	red pepper flakes
	salt

Build a good charcoal fire in one end of a large, long covered-wagon type grill. While the coals are getting hot, trim the fat from the hindquarter and bone it. Sprinkle the inside with salt and red pepper flakes. (Walter Allen says to go lightly on the salt, and I say to remember that dried red pepper is very hot stuff.) Place the bacon strips and the garlic in the open hindquarter. Then roll and tie the hindquarter with cotton string.

Place the rolled meat into a pan of suitable size, then pour in the Italian dressing and the wine. Arrange the sliced onion on top of the meat, then add the mushrooms, carrots, and potatoes to the pan. Cover loosely with aluminum foil. Place the pan on the grid, at the opposite end from the fire. Close the hood. Baste the meat from time to time with liquid from the pan—but don't open the hood too often, or for long periods of time, lest you lose too much heat. Cook the meat for about 4 hours, more or less, depending on how you like it, how big a chunk of meat you have, the size of your grill, and the fire. (The safest procedure is to use a good meat thermometer, although Walter Allen himself may not need one. I like my venison roasts cooked to 135 degrees or so on the inside, which will be medium rare.) You may have to add a little charcoal to the fire.

Purists may argue that red wine ought to be used instead of white. Frankly, I use whatever I've got on hand. I've even tried Heskett '90 and Hesket '87, a brew that a friend of mine makes each year from the juice of scuppernongs.

After our repast at Choctawhatchee Lodge that memorable night, sitting beside a fireside, Walter Allen told me that he really didn't consider his venison ham recipe to be either grilling or barbecuing. Nor do I. And it's obviously not smoking, since the meat is wrapped in foil. But it is a perfect example of cooking by the indirect method on a large covered grill. Obviously, a large grill is required simply because a whole hind leg of venison would fill up a small grill.

The large covered-wagon grill discussed above is really ideal for the patio because with it the expert chef can cook just about everything. If it has adjustable racks or fire grates, as most do, it will grill steaks and other meats to perfection. It is large enough to cook plenty of meat at one time, along with a few vegetables. By building the fire on one side of the grill and putting the meat on the other, it can be used for indirect cooking. Going a step further, adding wood to the fire will result in smoked-flavored meats.

One very nice thing about using these grills for indirect cooking is that the fire is easy to build and maintain. Start with a pile of briquets arranged between a couple of building bricks and the end. Light the briquets and leave them alone. There's no need to spread them out. The bricks can be moved about, permitting the use of a wider or bigger fire. For an added touch and a little smoke, use pieces of green hickory or other good wood to hold in the briquets. For this purpose, a segment of log cut to length and split into quarters will work best; put one flat side down and bank the fire with the other flat side. Also, most of the large grills are made of heavy-duty iron or steel, so that building a fire of wood or coal is certainly an option. And a good one, if you've got the time and the wood.

Of course, the better grills will have vents in the hood, draft controls at the firebox, doors to get into the fire box, and so on. A good temperature gauge that reads in degrees (instead of low-medium-high) is highly desirable.

A word of caution. Slow cooking in a large grill is not for those chefs who like to baste every two minutes. Opening the hood too often lets out the heat, just as surely as opening the door of an oven in the kitchen. It's best to put your meat down and leave it. Occasional basting is all right, but be quick about it. Actually, it's usually not necessary to turn the meat with indirect cooking, so that all the basting can be done on top and very quickly. This no-turn feature makes it very easy to deal with large pieces of meat, such as whole hams.

Usually, a drip pan is used under large chunks of meat, merely to prevent a mess in the bottom. Any sort of pan of suitable size can be used, with or without water in it. The pan is easy to use, since it merely sits on the empty side of the fire grate. The grates of the better units are very heavy, often made of cast iron, but are easily moved about with the aid of a special tool. Further, the grates are used in three or four sections.

One very nice feature of this type grill is that you can build a fire on one end, use it to grill steaks to perfection, and then put a roast on the other end, close the hood, and let it cook for several hours.

All in all, the large covered-wagon grill with heat control vents and adjustable racks is one of the most versatile cooking machines available. If I had to choose one type of grill, this would surely be it. Usually, however, these units are not cheap and are not always sold in mass-market discount houses. Look around; choose carefully. A really good one will last forever, with reasonable care.

Many people use two or more of these grills to cook for large crowds, or enjoy cooking large chunks of meat. Here are a few recipes:

Ike's Flank Steak & Bootsie's Marinade

My older brother gave me a recipe over the telephone for cooking a flank steak with the aid of his wife's marinade. "Do you know what a flank steak is?" he asked, like an older brother. "Of course," I said, hanging up the telephone and heading for my copy of Jack Ubaldi's *Meat Book*. "Flank Steak," according to Ubaldi, "is the fibrous muscle located on the inside wall of the beef flank. The meat is tender and juicy. It weighs 2 to 2½ pounds (hamburgers can be made with the trimmings). In selecting a flank steak, be sure it is short and thick, with some white fat on it. The long, lean flank steaks are generally of poor quality and will be chewy, with not much flavor." All in all, it's a piece of meat that benefits from long, slow indirect cooking, and, being juicy, it is ideal for this purpose. Here's what you'll need:

flank steak	3 or 4 drops Liquid Smoke
1 cup soy sauce	3 or 4 drops Tabasco sauce
1 cup Worcestershire sauce	1 teaspoon garlic powder
⅛ cup olive oil	salt and pepper to taste

112

Mix the soy sauce, Worcestershire sauce, olive oil, Liquid Smoke, Tabasco sauce, and garlic powder. Put the steak into a plastic Ziploc bag and pour the marinade mixture over it. Marinate in the refrigerator overnight or at least for several hours. Turn the bag over a couple of times.

When you are ready to cook, build a charcoal fire on one side of your grill. When the coals are ready, put the flank steak on the opposite side of the grill and close the cover. When the steak is almost done (after about an hour), move it directly over the coals and brown it on both sides. Salt and pepper the meat lightly on both sides, then let it rest for 5 or 6 minutes. Before serving, slice the steak thinly on a diagonal. The last point is quite important: This cut of meat should *always* be cut thinly and on a bias.

Slow Hawaiian Chicken Breasts

Here's another one from my brother, Colonel Ike Livingston, retired, who gave me the flank steak recipe above.

chicken breasts, skinned and boned	**⅓ cup olive oil**
pineapple slices	**⅓ cup brown sugar**
⅓ cup pineapple juice (saved from the slices)	**2 cloves garlic, crushed**
	1 teaspoon freshly grated ginger root
⅓ cup sherry	**salt and pepper**

Mix the pineapple juice, sherry, olive oil, brown sugar, garlic, and ginger root. Put the chicken into a plastic Ziploc bag and marinate it overnight, turning the bag several times. Cook very slowly in a covered grill until the chicken is almost done. Baste once or twice with the marinade, and sprinkle lightly with salt and pepper. (The exact cooking time will vary, depending on your fire and the size of your grill, but allow at least an hour.) For the last few minutes, put the pineapple slices directly over the coals, browning both sides. Serve the pineapple slices with the chicken.

Jamaican-style Beef

Here's a good recipe that calls for a "barbecue" rub that is popular in Jamaica. The recipe for the rub paste, set forth on page 176, lists rum as optional. I recommend that it be used with beef.

6-pound rump roast, rolled
1 tablespoon oil
1 cup jerk rub paste

Several hours before cooking, coat the roast with oil and rub it with the jerk paste. Use all of the oil and jerk rub, then put the roast into a plastic bag and refrigerate overnight, or at least for several hours. When you are ready to cook, build a fire in one side of your grill and put the roast in the other side. It's best to put the roast into a baking pan, then pour over it any juice that might have accumulated in the plastic bag. Cover the grill and cook it for an hour. Then quickly turn the roast, rolling it in the pan juice. Cook for another hour or so, basting it with pan juice every 15 or 20 minutes. It's best to use a good meat thermometer inserted into the roast. For rare meat, cook until the thermometer reaches 135 to 140 degrees, then let it sit for a few minutes. Slice and serve with the pan juice.

Stuffed Turkey

I like to start this recipe with a good turkey of about 15 pounds dressed weight. Usually, my wife or I make a cornbread dressing for the stuffing, then top this at the table with a gravy made with the giblets. I also cut off the wings for use in the dressing, as these usually cook too long and complicate the carving.

> **1 15-pound turkey**
> **oil or bacon drippings**
> **salt**
> **stuffing** (your favorite)

Cut the wings off the turkey and save them, along with the neck and giblets, for the stuffing. Build a fire in one side of your grill, grease the far end of the grid, close the hood, and bring the temperature up to 325 degrees. Coat the turkey with oil, salt it inside and out, then stuff it loosely. Truss it if you like. Tie the legs close to tail end of the body with cotton twine. Put the bird into the grill on the end opposite from the fire. Close the hood. While the bird starts cooking, make the following basting sauce:

> **1 cup white wine**   **2 cloves garlic, minced**
> **½ cup olive oil**   **1 tablespoon salt**
> **¼ cup chopped fresh**   **1 teaspoon pepper**
>   **parsley or 2 tablespoons**   **1 teaspoon paprika**
>   **dry flakes**   **1 teaspoon rosemary**
> **1 large onion, peeled and**
>   **diced**

Mix all the sauce ingredients in a pan. Bring to heat and simmer for about 20 minutes. Baste the turkey with the sauce every 30 minutes or so during cooking. After cooking for 2 or 3 hours, cut the cotton cord so that the legs are loose. Cook for a total of about 20 minutes per pound. Five hours or so for a 15-pound turkey. When the bird is done, the leg joint moves easily in the socket. For best results, use a meat thermometer or "button." Allow plenty of time to cook the bird. If the temperature in your grill drops, you'll have to add to the cooking time drastically.

Note: This technique can also be used to smoke a turkey. Omit the sauce and baste the bird with bacon drippings from time to time. Add hickory chunks or green wood to the fire.

Kabayaki

Grilled or smoked eel is a favorite in many parts of the world, but, unfortunately, many Americans don't take advantage of this excellent fish. (Part of the problem is that the eel no doubt got a bad name in America because it is none too good when fried, which was the American way with fish until quite recently.) My recipe is based on a popular Japanese dish, except that I merely skin the eel instead of trying to flatten it. Since the eel is very oily and can stand long cooking, I use a combination of direct and indirect heat. The Japanese bone the eel and then keep it open and flat with skewers. I merely cut mine in pieces of about 6 inches. They can be left whole, but somehow the image is too snake-like to suit most people.

> **eels or lampreys**
> **I cup soy sauce**
> **I cup saké or sherry**
> **½ cup dark brown sugar**

Skin your eels and cut them into pieces. Mix a marinade of soy sauce, saké, and brown sugar. Pour the marinade over the eel and refrigerate (in a nonmetallic container) for several hours. When you are ready to cook, build a hot fire on one side of your grill. Cook the eels for a few minutes on both sides, then baste with marinade and move them to the side away from the heat. Close the hood and cook the eel for 1 to 2 hours, depending to some extent on the thickness of the pieces. Test a large piece with a fork before serving.

Eels should be kept very fresh until they are cooked, and the best ones are kept alive until the last moment—but this practice is seldom practical for most Americans, unless they have a spare bathtub and a very understanding spouse. The lamprey isn't an eel, but it is similar and can be cooked in the same way.

This dish is good when cooked on a grill, especially when using a wood fire beside a stream. Delicious smoked eels can also be made by the recipe above by merely adding some wood chips to the coals during the indirect cooking phase. Although the recipe above is for the large covered-wagon grills, it's easy to cook the eels in a silo cooker, with or without smoke and with or without water in the drip pan. Usually, cooking for about 4 hours at about 160 degrees will be just right, especially if you baste a couple of times during the process. Very large eels may require longer cooking.

Of course eels are not to everybody's taste, and should be served along with some other type of meat if you've got squeamish folk to feed. I suggest that you cook another meat that requires about the same cooking time.

BARREL OR DRUM GRILLS

Possibly more good meat has been turned out on a large home-made grill than any other kind. I'm talking about the old barrel grill, made by cutting a 55-gallon metal drum in half lengthwise and then fitting it back together with hinges. A rack is placed inside for the meat, and, sometimes, a fire grate is added. Some even have doors and vents. The big advantage of such units is size. They can be used to grill a hundred hamburgers, or they can be closed and used to cook a large ham and a turkey, by the indirect method.

The large covered wagon grills, built to last, are quite versatile and can be used for direct grilling, indirect cooking, and smoking.

But, alas, the problem with such grills is that they are hard to move about. If left outside, they tend to rust out. The relatively thin metal also tends to burn out. The CB940, by contrast, has wheels and can be moved into the garage or other storage area, and is made of heavy-duty metal. Another problem with barrel grills is that they sometimes don't fit back together quite right, have wobbly legs, and, in general, lack eye appeal. Again, however, let me say that they can cook up some wonderful meats, and are large enough to cook such go-withs as corn on the cob.

You can't buy one of these units in stores, but usually some local metalworker can make one for you. Although the total cost of a custom rig may well exceed the price a large covered-wagon unit, some good ol' boys will cook on nothing else. Down in Jamaica, such grills are used extensively in jerk stands, either because of economic necessity or to impress the tourists.

A neat two-barrel unit called the Hondo is manufactured out in Texas. It features a large heavy-duty barrel, made pretty much as described above. The large barrel has a grid for the meat and an adjustable grate for the fire. The hood is hinged, of course, and a smokestack vent is stationary. In addition, the Hondo has a smaller barrel-shaped unit, essentially a firebox, attached to the main barrel. The smaller unit is dropped down somewhat, so that its top right corner fits onto the bottom left corner of the larger barrel. The small barrel also has a firebox, a grid, an adjustable air-intake door, fuel door, and hood. Thus, a fire can be built in the small bottom unit and the meat put into the top unit for indirect cooking and smoking. The firebox unit burns wood or charcoal for up to 8 hours, and, since the firebox is offset, there is no danger of flare-ups or fire. Nice. Very nice. Of course, either the bottom unit or the top unit, or both, can be used for direct grilling with or without the use of the hood. All in all, the Hondo is a great design for grilling and indirect cooking, and it also works very nicely for smoking. *Hondo* is Spanish for "big and deep." It has a cooking grid area of 743 square inches. Although the unit was designed for cooking for a crowd, the offset firebox makes it practical to grill a couple of steaks.

The Hondo, a Texas-made refinement of the old 55-gallon drum, is ideal for grilling large and small batches of meat, for indirect cooking, and for smoking and barbecuing.

BIG TANK GRILLS

When I first saw the cooker in my neighbor's back yard early one morning, I thought that Ol' Dan Webster had bought himself a small train engine. It was about 6 feet long, 3 or 4 feet in diameter, and had a smoke stack on one end. The smell of hickory smoke and meat was in the air and it didn't take me long to realize that Dan was cooking.

The large tank was mounted on a small boat trailer, and in it Dan was smoke-cooking a huge batch of chicken for a meeting of the Henry County Auburn University Club. By "large" batch, I mean 92 chicken halves. That's 46 chickens.

Dan cooked all day, checking the meat from time to time, and I stayed away until about sundown, when I could no longer stand the wonderful aroma of smoke and cooked meat. "The secret of it," Dan said, raising the hood of the thing, "is in cooking the chicken for a long time." Off the top of the pile of chicken, he took a piece and popped it open. "It'll get a little more tender in a while, but you can eat it now," he said, handing both halves to me. I took the leg quarter and bit into it. Well, I don't know how it could have been more tender—or better. It was still very juicy, and done all the way to the bone.

After finishing off the leg quarter, I licked my fingers and started on the breast end while looking over Dan's cooking rig, which, he said, had been borrowed from a local bank. The tank had been cut in half and hinged, with a locking mechanism for holding it open. It had a smoke stack on one end and a firebox door on the other. The grid fitted in just below the hinge line. Perfect. It even had a rake for moving the coals about. For easy portability, it had been welded onto a small boat trailer. I don't have a blueprint, but any good welder should be able to construct one from a suitable tank. Of course, such a cooker can be used for cooking up hams and all manner of large pieces of meat. Of, if you want to feed chicken to a hundred folks, you may want to try the following:

Dan's Auburn Club Chicken

For this recipe, Dan buys chicken halves from a wholesale meat firm instead of buying whole birds. That way, he says, he doesn't have any giblets to mess with. Further, he says he buys grain-fed birds, not those that have been fattened on mash.

92 chicken halves
2 bottles Dale's steak sauce (16-ounce size)
2 bottles vinegar (32-ounce size)
1 bottle lemon juice (32-ounce size)
1 jar lemon-pepper seasoning salt (2½ ounces)
1 small bottle garlic juice (2-ounce)
20 to 30 pounds of charcoal briquets
2 to 3 pounds hickory in chunks or green wood wheels

The night before you are ready to cook, put the hickory chunks into a tub and pour water over them. Let the chunks soak until day, turning them over at about midnight. Also at midnight, mix a marinade. In a pitcher with a good pouring spout, mix the steak sauce, vinegar, lemon juice, lemon-pepper, and garlic juice. This will be used for both a marinade and a basting sauce, and will be poured from the pitcher into a squirt bottle as needed.

At about daylight the next morning, trim the chicken halves while they are still very cold, removing the tail and large blobs of fat. Place a layer of chicken into an ice chest and squirt on some of the marinade. Add another layer of chicken and more marinade. Repeat until the ice chest is full. Use as many ice chests as needed. Marinate the chicken for at least 2 hours.

Build a charcoal fire in the cooker, using about 10 pounds of briquets. The fire should run from one end of the cooker to the other. When the coals are hot, fill the grid with chicken halves, packing closely but not overlapping. (Dan's rig held about 70 chicken halves, which complicated his cooking since he had 92 pieces to cook. We'll get to that later.) Put a few hickory chunks on the edge of the fire, on the opposite end from the smoke stack. Close the hood and cook for two hours, adding a few pieces of hickory at the end, as needed. (The hickory can be added through a door without opening the hood.) Note that the initial fuel burns out and the heat is maintained only by a small fire at the end of the unit, which can be attended through a little door at the end. Note also that chunk charcoal works better than briquets, simply because it contains no binders or other additives.

After about two hours, raise the hood and turn the chicken halves. Squirt a little of the sauce onto each piece of chicken. Close the hood and add more hickory chunks if needed. Also add a little more charcoal if needed.

Cook for two hours. Turn the chicken halves and squirt each one with basting sauce. Add charcoal to the fire if needed, and add more hickory chunks to the end, building up quite a bit of smoke. Check, turn, and baste the chicken every 30 minutes until it is done. When done, you should be able to cut into a piece down to the bone without seeing pinkish juice. (Remember, however, that the chicken will be cooked a little more, since you have 92 pieces in all.) When the chicken seems done, pile it on the far end, away from the hickory chips, and rake all the coals to the other half of the cooker. Put the rest of the chicken onto the grid directly over the coals. Cook the same as the first batch.

When all the chicken is done, pile it on the rack in one end of the cooker as far away from the fire as possible. If you've got a few coals left, add a little more hickory wood for smoke. Close the hood and the vents until you are ready to serve. It's best if the chicken stays in a pile for at least 30 minutes. It will finish cooking slowly, without losing any juice, and should be tender enough to fall apart in your hand when you pop it at the joint.

If you will be serving the chicken away from the cooker, pack it into the ice chests. It will stay hot for hours.

This chicken can be served in a number of ways. If you want something simple, try it with cold potato salad and rolls, served on a paper plate with a plastic fork. Try beer or iced tea.

KETTLE GRILLS

Many recipes in books and magazines call for a drip pan under the meat. More often than not, the reference is to a kettle-ype grill with a cover. Typically, a charcoal fire is built in the center of the unit. When the coals get right, they are scattered around the edge of the kettle, doughnut shaped, and a round pan or other container is placed in the middle. The meat is, of course, centered above the drip pan. Usually, a little water is poured into the pan.

As a rule, the drip pan method provides a neat solution for grilling fatty meats, such as the Boston butt or a domestic duck, which would cause lots of burnt grease smoke, or fires, if placed directly above the coals.

Normally, the meat is cooked by a combination of direct heat (radiant heat from the coals) and convective heat (hot air, as in a kitchen oven). Frequent basting is not recommended when using this technique, since opening the hood will allow the heat to escape. Ideally, the drip pan method works best with fatty meats that do not require basting.

Judging by the number of recipes in books and magazines, one would suspect that the drip pan method is a favorite way of cooking in America. It's true that the kettle-shaped grill, usually inexpensive, is very, very popular. The authors of one cookbook of my acquaintance noted that *all* of the recipes in the book were cooked on a kettle grill. This is fine, if everyone who buys the book also happens to own a kettle grill (of the same size). Or if everyone who dips into the book for a recipe or two also reads the front matter, in which the use of the kettle grill is explained. In any case, the use of the drip pan is sometimes not as versatile as it might at first seem. While cooking a turkey breast, for example, you may run out of fire. In this case, do you build a doughnut fire, or do you take out the drip pan and start a new fire in the middle? Do you take out the hot rack to add coals? Obviously, a large covered-wagon unit simply doesn't present as many problems.

Finally, let me say that the drip pan method in a kettle grill will surely work—but, frankly, I've never known anyone who actually used it on a regular basis. Instead, most chefs prefer to pile a fire on one side of the unit instead of using a toroidal, or doughnut-shaped arrangement. I don't have firm statistics on this matter, however, and I don't intend to discourage the use of the kettle grill in any way. For the price, it's a fine unit. But it's really not as versatile as the large covered-wagon grills.

If you are shopping around for a kettle grill, I recommend that you get a large one if you plan to do lots of indirect grilling or if you want to cook large chunks of meat. In a small unit, a drip pan will take up too much room.

Here are a couple of recipes to try:

Citrus Stuffed Duck

Because the domestic duck contains lots of fat, it really should be cooked over a drip pan. The technique used in this recipe can be applied to other birds, but remember that duck breasts are quite thin, as compared to chicken; that is why, in the directions below, the duck leg quarters are cooked for 10 minutes before the breast is added.

> **1 4½- – 5-pound domestic duck**
> **4 orange slices, ⅛ inch thick**
> **4 lemon slices, ⅛ inch thick**
> **fresh thyme, or packaged**
> **1 teaspoon salt**
> **1 teaspoon pepper**

Build a fire in your kettle grill. While waiting for it to come to heat, cut the wings off the duck and save them, along with the giblets, for making giblet gravy or some such recipe. With a sharp knife, cut off the duck leg quarters. (Go carefully, remembering that the joints on a duck are much farther forward than on a chicken.) Using poultry shears, cut down the center of the duck's back, then lay open the breast. Carefully work your finger between the skin and the flesh of the duck's breast, and of both leg quarters, making pockets for the stuffing. Do not completely remove the skin along the edges. On the leg quarters, work only on the side with the most skin and start where the thigh joined the back. You may have to cut some of the membrane here and there with the shears or a sharp fillet knife. Next, mince the thyme and put it into a plate. (Packaged thyme can be used instead if you don't have fresh.) Mix in the salt and pepper. Dip the orange and lemon slices into the mixture, coating both sides. Stuff the orange and lemon slices between the skin and the meat of the duck breast, using 2 slices of each for the breast and 1 slice of each of the leg quarters.

When the coals are ready, spread them out around the edge of the firebox and put a drip pan in the middle. Place the duck leg quarters onto the grid (skin side up) over the drip pan. Close the hood and cook for 10 minutes. Open the hood and quickly place the duck breast on the grid between the two leg quarters. All the meat should be over the drip pan. Close the hood quickly and cook for 15 minutes, or until the meat is done and the skin is crisply golden. The exact cooking times depends on the size of the duck and the heat of the fire. If in doubt, cut into one of the thighs all the way to the bone to see if it is too bloody. Duck is best when cooked rare or at least medium rare. Before serving, cut the breast in half lengthwise.

I allow half a duck per person. Before planning this recipe, remember that you'll need a large kettle grill if you plan to cook more than one duck at the same time. You can gain some space by cutting the breast piece (bone in) away from the back.

Stuffed Cornish Game Hens

These birds, besides being delicious, are ideal for a kettle grill because the cooking time is just right for a charcoal fire that surrounds a drip pan. Also, the birds fit compactly on the grill so that several of them can be cooked. I allow one bird for each person. Heavy eaters may require more, but remember that the wild rice stuffing is also quite filling.

STUFFING:
½ cup wild rice
2 cups chicken broth
½ envelope onion soup mix
1 cup mushrooms, chopped
1 tablespoon chopped fresh parsley
salt and pepper

It's best to make the stuffing and the basting sauce in the kitchen before you are ready to fire up the grill. To prepare the stuffing, heat the broth in a saucepan, add the rice, bring to a boil, reduce heat, cover, and simmer for 1 hour. Stir in the mushrooms, parsley, onion soup mix, salt, and pepper. Simmer for 10 minutes, stirring from time to time. Pour off any liquid.

BASTING SAUCE:
1 cup orange marmalade
¼ cup dark brown sugar
¼ cup rice vinegar
1 tablespoon grated fresh ginger root
2 teaspoons soy sauce
salt
pepper

To prepare the basting sauce, mix all ingredients and heat in a pan. As soon as the mixture starts to bubble, immediately reduce the heat and simmer for a few minutes, stirring constantly. Do not bring to a hard boil. Keep the sauce warm until you are ready to cook.

4 to 6 rock Cornish game hens
melted butter

Build a charcoal fire in the kettle grill. Back in the kitchen, brush the birds inside and out with melted butter. Stuff the birds loosely with the hot rice mixture. Trussing isn't necessary. Tie the wings and the legs to the body of the bird with cotton twine. When the charcoal is ready, rig with a drip pan. Baste the birds all over and place them, breast up, on the rack over the drip pan. Cover and cook for 30 minutes. Then quickly baste the breasts of the birds, keeping the hood open no longer than necessary. Baste again every 10 minutes until the birds are done. The total cooking time will be 1 hour, more or less, depending on your grill and your fire.

Variation: Substitute a marmalade made from the bitter (Seville) orange.

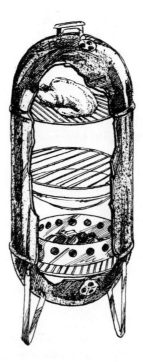

The silo cooker, usually rigged with a water pan and a wood-chip box, is very easy to use for indirect cooking and for smoking.

SILO COOKERS

These units are often called smoker/cookers or water/smokers or some such name with a slash in it. I call them silo cookers simply because they look like miniature silos; this comparison holds especially true for the popular two-rack units. By whatever name, these units are quite easy to use and are about as foolproof as outside cooking can get. There are several models on the market, but essentially they have the following features: a firebox or heating element on the bottom, a small pan for holding wood chips atop the heat, a large water pan a few inches above the heat, a cooking rack about half way up the silo, another cooking rack in the top part of the silo, and a domed lid. (Some models have only one cooking rack, and others are modular or stackable.) Usually, the lid doesn't have a hinge, simply because it's difficult to put a single hinge on thin metal and expect it to hold up. Some do have some sort of clamp mechanism that helps hold the lid. These units have a temperature gauge, which is quite an important feature, especially on those that burn charcoal. I prefer a gauge that reads in degrees instead of such scale as warm-medium-hot. Even with the best gauge, however, remember that heat rises and that the top rack will get hotter than the middle rack. So, if you are cooking two pieces of meat of equal size, the one on top will get done first. Also remember that large pieces of meat should also be cooked with the aid of a meat thermometer.

Most of these units are relatively inexpensive, and of course they are made of thin metal and wire racks. Some of the more expensive silo units made with stainless steel are a little better and fit together with more precision. Similar Oriental models, such as the Kamado, are made from ceramic material. These are usually quite attractive and do a very good job, but they are also expensive—and breakable.

Most of these units either burn charcoal or use an electrical coil for heat. Gas-burning models have been introduced, but do not seem to have caught on. The charcoal units are satisfactory, but remember that large pieces of meat will require long cooking times, which means that the fire will burn out if it isn't kept up. (As a rule, the larger units will burn much longer than the smaller units.) One big advantage of the electric units is that they will heat all day or all night—at the same temperature. But remember that the wind temperatures outside will have a bearing on the exact cooking times; sometimes this influence can be considerable, simply because the units, especially the two-rack models, have a large surface exposed to the air.

All of these silo units have a water pan between the center rack and the heat source. Its purpose is to catch drippings from the meat and to provide a source of moisture. The moisture—often mixed with smoke from wood chips—is an advantage when cooking meat that tends to be dry, such as turkey breast and venison roasts.

Partly because of the moisture and partly because of the slow cooking, a silo cooker with electric heat is the most foolproof of all the outdoor cookers. If the manufacturer's instructions are followed, it's hard to go wrong with these units. I do, however, feel that some writers have gone out on a limb by recommending the use of wine and other expensive liquids for the water pan. I've read instructions for pouring a whole quart of wine into the water pan. This, to me, is a waste of money—or wine—or both. When you pour wine into the water pan, most of the flavor stays in the pan and doesn't rise to the meat. If the pan liquid (including the meat drippings) is to be used in making a sauce or gravy, then wine might be justified. Some people marinate the meat before cooking, then put the leftover marinade into the water pan. It won't hurt a thing, but how much its vapor will add to the meat is open to question. But this is one man's opinion, and future chefs may have special stuff to put into water pans and thereby flavor the meat, much like Vicks is used in steam vaporizers.

Although most people use silo cookers for adding smoke flavor to meat—indeed, they are often called smokers or smoker/cookers—the smoke part doesn't necessarily have to be used, as indicated below.

Succulent Beef Roast

Some women cook a roast to death in the kitchen oven, and of course cooking a roast too long makes the meat difficult to chew and swallow. Knowledgeable chefs will put a roast beef in a covered roasting pan and add a little water to it, which will provide some water vapor to keep the meat moist. The silo cooker will accomplish the same thing, and the electric unit can in fact be used in the kitchen (without smoke) as well as on the patio.

10 pound roast beef (or smaller)	**2 cloves garlic**
	2 bay leaves
2 cups good red wine	**1 tablespoon salt**
1 cup beef stock	**1 teaspoon black pepper**
1 medium onion	

Heat the wine and beef stock. Chop the onion and add it to the liquid, along with bay leaves, salt, pepper, and 1 clove of the garlic, minced. Put the roast into a large nonmetallic bowl (or other container) and refrigerate it for 24 hours. Retain the marinade. Shortly before cooking, peel the other garlic clove and split it in half. With a long, thin knife, make 2 slits in the roast, spaced well apart, and insert the split pieces of garlic.

Put the meat into the top rack of the silo cooker, and pour the marinade into the water pan. Add water. Cook for 10 hours, more or less, on low heat. Turn and baste with pan drippings every hour or so, and add water to the pan as needed. The exact cooking times will vary. A meat thermometer inserted into the roast is your best guide. The larger the roast, the more important a thermometer becomes. Try 140 degrees for medium rare.

Easy Hams

One of the best things you can do with a "cooked" or "cured" ham that you purchase at the grocery store is to put it into a silo unit for long cooking. These days, even "smoked" hams are cured by pumping stuff into them, including water. Long, slow cooking in a large, covered grill will improve the flavor and the texture of such a ham—and cook out the water that was pumped into it. Either a shank portion or a butt portion can be used, or go for the whole thing. It's hard to cook one of these too long, and after 7 or 8 hours it will be ready to fall off the bone. No seasoning is necessary, but some mustard and pepper won't hurt a thing. And stick a few cloves into the meat here and there. These hams will drip quite a bit, so make sure that the water pan is in place.

High/Low Cooking

It's easy to cook two different kinds of meat in a silo unit that has double racks. Put the fatty piece on top and the lean piece on the bottom to catch the drippings. For example, put a turkey breast on the bottom rack and Boston butt on top. Or a venison roast on the bottom and a domestic duck on top. Remember that the top piece of meat will cook hotter, so that you may have to take it out of the unit before the bottom gets done. If in doubt, trust in a meat thermometer.

The recipe below is just typical of such arrangements. Also try a domestic duck or a fat goose on top and a large venison roast on bottom.

> **I cured ham, butt or shank portion**
> **I large turkey breast**
> **salt and pepper**

Salt and pepper the ham and the turkey breast. Start the fire or turn on the electrical heat. Fill the pan with water. Put the turkey breast in the center of the middle rack. Put the ham in the center of the top rack. Cook until the turkey is ready. No basting or turning will be necessary, although I do like to turn the ham at least once and sprinkle both pieces of meat with salt and pepper. If the ham starts to fall off the bone, take it out and finish cooking the turkey without it.

Note: The ham indicated above is a typical supermarket ham, as discussed in the previous recipe. Fresh hams can also be used to advantage.

Part Four

SMOKING

Not many years ago, smoking was a means of preserving meat, usually accomplished by hanging the meat, after it has been cured in salt, for a long time in wood smoke at a temperature of less than 100 degrees. The process was especially well adapted to curing fish and pork. Most of the "smoked" pork in the modern supermarket, however, is cured by injecting it with preservatives and an artificial smoke flavor. A few people have constructed their own smokehouses and can cold-smoke meat at home, but these days most of us "smoke" meat in a covered barbecue grill (or silo unit), using charcoal briquets for heat and wood chips for flavor. The meat is really cooked as usual, with the addition of smoke.

Because no amount of smoke can save the day for meat that isn't properly cooked, the novice would do well to master the techniques of grilling and indirect cooking set forth in Parts Two and Three, then apply smoke, more or less, as a bonus to flavor and aroma.

THE KINDS OF SMOKE

As the old moonshiners knew, a fire built with dry, well-seasoned wood doesn't put out much smoke. Green, freshly-cut wood, on the other hand, is a dead giveaway to the location of one's still, although it might be ideal for sending signals to another valley—or for smoking sausage. Most of the packaged wood chips or chunks on the market are, of course, quite dry and are usually soaked in water before use. But soaked wood is not the same as green wood. It's really not. Green or seasoned, a number of good woods can be used for smoking meat, and many of these can be gathered easily from woods and fencerows. Here are a few to try:

HICKORY. My father and his father before him used green, freshly cut hickory wood to smoke and cure hams, sausage, and other meats. And of course dried hickory chips and chunks are favorites all over the South for modern day smoking on the patio. I may be disowned by the rest of my family, and may be run out of my native Southeast, but I dare to suggest that the reputation of hickory may owe much to the fact that it simply burns for a long time. During the days of the farm smokehouses, the meat was often smoked for two or three weeks, and of course nobody wanted to get up in the middle of the night to tend the fire. Thus, a green wood that burned for a long time and made lots of good-smelling smoke was highly desirable. Hickory was just right. Green hickory logs and cut wood are still used to great advantage both as a fuel and as a smoking agent by knowledgeable amateurs as well as professionals.

HICKORY NUTS. A Georgia cracker who visited me recently told me about smoking fish with hickory nuts. He gathers the nuts in autumn or early winter and stores them in a dry place. Then he soaks them for a day or two before using them for smoking purposes.

ALDER. Popular in the Pacific Northwest and some other areas, alder chips and chunks are packaged and sold all over the nation. Those who prefer it say that its smoke is ideal for fish and poultry. Some of the best salmon that I've eaten was smoked with alder, but in all honesty I'll have to add that it was prepared in a long, slow process made with green alder wood.

GUAVA. A favorite smoking wood in Hawaii, the guava tree grows in southern Florida and other tropical or subtropical regions. It's a small tree, sometimes not much more than a bush, that has dry, hard wood. The fruit of the guava is eaten out of hand, and makes wonderful jelly.

OTHER FRUIT TREES. A good many people in the Northeast and elsewhere swear by apple wood for smoking. Others say that wild crabapple is the stuff to use. In Florida, many people use green citrus trees as a smoking agent. Pear trees and plum also make good smoke. And cherry.

PECAN TREES. I use more pecan than any other kind of wood simply because it is readily available to me. I merely snip or saw off a branch or two from one of my trees. Some of the limbs hang too low anyway. Normally, I use green, freshly cut wood, but of course it can also be dried for several months and then soaked in water before cooking time.

PECAN HULLS. Anyone who has ever burned pecan hulls know that they make lots of smoke. Now they are being packaged and marketed for smoking meat. If you want lots of smoke fast, try them.

OLIVE PITS. Olive pits are said to be a well-kept Spanish secret for adding a smoke flavor to grilled seafood. The secret is out, and I have seen packages of Mediterranean olive "chips" listed in mail-order catalogs at fancy prices. Also, briquets made from olive pits and wood are available.

CORNCOBS. In years past, corncobs were often used for fuel as well as for smoking meats. They tend to blaze up, however, and should be watched carefully. I'm sure that purists will have opinions on whether the white cob or the red is better for smoking and perhaps other purposes.

SASSAFRAS. I sometimes smoke meat with green sassafras wood, which is quite abundant on most fencerows in my part of the country. I like the smell of it. The aromatic oil of sassafras comes mainly from the roots and bark, and I am fond of drinking a tea made by boiling the roots in water. For smoking, however, I usually strip the bark off a limb or trunk, then chop the wood into chunks or fingers. The wood is very hard and makes good fence posts. At one time, it was used for railroad crossties and in making chicken coops.

When you gather a little sassafras for smoking or for tea, get a few green leaves. Dry them, crush them in a mortar, and use the powder (very sparingly) to thicken soups and gumbos. The American Indians knew this, and the powder is now marketed in spice sections under the name of filé. The oldtimers also used sassafras as a herb by cutting the wood or root into slivers and inserting them into the meat. I like it in a fresh pork, and I have used it to advantage when hot smoking a Boston butt. Try a piece about the size of a pencil, pointed on the end, stuck right into the meat.

MESQUITE. This small tree has always been popular in parts of the Southwest, where it grows, and now the stuff is being shipped all over the world. I've even got an Alaskan camp recipe that calls for mesquite! As a smoke, it is certainly good—but not *that* good. Its early reputation came as a fuel, not as a flavoring agent. The wood makes hot coals and lasts a long time.

The mesquite tree grows better in hot, dry areas, and it has a root that is often longer than the tree is tall. At one time, the wood was used for making railroad ties. After that, owners of mesquite thickets weren't laughing when they went to the bank—until the smoking craze started and the smell of mesquite wafted across the land from the tropics in the south of Florida to the tundra in the north of the Yukon.

MANGROVE AND PALMETTO. In Florida, the mangrove tree has come under environmental pressure from developers and jackleg chefs. The wood of the mangrove is said to be ideal for smoking fish—especially mullet. I've also read that palmetto roots make good smoke, and that it is a favorite in some quarters. In the West, manzanita roots are sometimes used and touted.

OAK. Although not very popular, hardwood oak (deciduous) neverthe-less makes a very good smoke. Gather a few limbs and use them green for smoking, or chop and dry some chips and chunks the next time you cut a cord or two of firewood. Remember that green wood splits easier than dry or seasoned wood. When used as a fuel, dry oak makes a hot, long-lasting fire and good coals—and doesn't pop as badly as hickory. Green oak is hard to burn, which makes it good choice for smoking along with another fuel or source of heat. But oak doesn't make a lot of smoke, so that you have to use more of it if you want a strong flavor. Just because it isn't used in lots of recipes or listed in American catalogs that cater to patio chefs, don't count it out. I recently learned that it is used in Scotland to smoke salmon—and Scottish salmon, the ad said, is a favorite in Buckingham Palace.

WHISKEY KEGS. The reverend Elijah Craig was surprised when he discovered that moonshine whiskey stored in charred oak barrels tasted good. This was the beginning of Bourbon. The good reverend would no doubt also be surprised to learn that meat smoked with whiskey barrel chunks is also quite tasty. But the purists may want to point out that there is the Kentucky bourbon barrel and then there is the Tennessee sour mash whiskey barrel. Although both barrels may be made from white oak and charred by the same technique, remember that true Tennessee whiskey is filtered through a sugar maple charcoal before it is put into the charred oak barrels. Surely you can taste the difference!

While on this topic, I must point out that wine barrels have also been used to cook meat over an open fire. The meat? Rats. They were eaten in large numbers during the siege of Paris in 1870, and apparently the meat gained favor among the coopers, who skinned the rats, marinated them in oil and shallots, and grilled them over a fire made of broken wine barrels. In case any modern practitioner who wants to serve the dish to guests, he should know that it was properly called "Cooper Entrecôte."

GRAPEVINE CUTTINGS. The first time I heard about smoking with grape vines, I got my pruning shears and headed for the Choctawhatchee River, where I gather wild muscadines in season. Within a short time I had an armful of vines about ½ inch around, and with them I smoked some hamburgers and other good eats. In case you don't know a grape vine from a rope, the cuttings are available in packages, and are sometimes used dry to provide lots of smoke to foods that are cooked quickly.

PIMENTO. In Jamaica, the wood of the allspice tree, called pimento, is used for making the local barbecue called jerk. The tree grows wild on some of the islands of the Caribbean. Traditionally, the Jamaicans use the wood as a source of heat, but these days charcoal briquets are often used along with chips of pimento. The tree is a kind of myrtle—an evergreen—which is generally considered to be a no-no in smoke cookery. But the myrtle is also used, along with juniper, to smoke meat on the island of Sardinia.

OTHER WOODS. Most any good hardwood—such as walnut, maple, chestnut, beech, sweet bay, ash, or birch—can be used to advantage for making smoke. I wouldn't hesitate to use chinquapin, for example, and some beachcombers use driftwood without knowing exactly what it is. But be warned that some woods pop mightily, and anyone who throws a handful of catalpa wood chunks into a hot fire will think that somebody slipped in a pack of firecrackers!

COMBINATIONS. It was, of course, inevitable that many chefs would start blending woods for the perfect smoke. A fellow by the name of Greg R. Alexander had a recipe in *The South Carolina Wildlife Cookbook,* and in it he said, "I prefer smoking with one third hickory, one third oak, and one third fruit tree (plum). Add a few springs of rosemary, marjoram, or sage to the coals for an extra touch." Which brings up another topic:

HERBS AND SPICES. Some peoples of the world, especially in North Africa, use many kinds of spice and herbs for sprinkling onto a fire. Packaged grilling herbs are available in America, and, of course, you've got to purchase a different blend for fish, beef, and poultry.

Before moving on to your own mixes, you might profit by experimenting with bay leaves during one cookout, then with thyme, rosemary, etc., either fresh or dried. Remember that the Chinese chefs sometimes use tea leaves and pine needles for smoke-flavoring food. The list can be long, the combinations endless.

Personally, I usually put whatever spices and herbs that I want onto the meat or into a marinade or basting sauce. I prefer the robust smell of meat on the grill to that of incense or smoldering potpourri. But of course I allow and even cater to other opinions—especially in matters related to the perfumed garden.

141

A glance back over the list of smoking agents above should convince anyone that it doesn't make much difference which kind of hardwood is used. The person with an average sense of taste can discern only a slight difference of flavor, if any at all, in meat smoked with this or that good hardwood. Even if there is a difference, one flavor will probably be just as palatable as another. Just the other day I was arguing this point with my neighbor, Dan Webster, who gets excited about culinary matters, and I told him, I said, "Dan, cook us up twin tenderloins of pork on two separate but identical grills, both with the same kind of heat, for the exact same length of time, using, say, mesquite on the one and, say, chinquapin on the other. If you can tell the difference, I'll eat both of 'em."

I'm not saying that smoke isn't important. It is. For brute, primitive stimulation of the taste buds, nothing in the culinary world beats the smell of meat grilling over mesquite in El Paso, alder in Seattle, hickory in Tullahoma, or pimento in Jamaica. But I am, however, certain that the quality of the meat and the technique of cooking are much more important than the *specific* kind of wood that was used to make the smoke. Further, the materials that make the smoke may or may not have an influence on the flavor of the meat—but the choice of material does bear heavily on the mind, which in turn can influence the taste buds. Anyone who has cooked over smoldering camel or buffalo chips, for example, will tell you right quick that the food ought to be cooked in a pot and covered with a tight lid.

I know a fellow who works at a large wood chip plant, where hardwood logs are piled up as high as a mountain. Giant claws pick them up like toothpicks and feed them—whole logs—into huge jaws of steel. Out come the chips, blown directly into railroad cars. Carload after carload after carload, ton upon ton, they leave this part of the country, going somewhere. Does he take home a few chips for smoking meat on the patio? No. He likes chunks, not chips. And there is a difference.

CHIPS are thin pieces of wood that char away rather quickly. They are usually used on a fire when quick smoke is needed for a short period of time. They are ideal for direct grilling over hot coals.

CHUNKS are much larger and thicker than chips. When dry, these are usually smoked in water and then placed on or next to a low fire for a long cooking time. They are ideal for use in slow cooking.

TWIGS AND SHAVINGS are small pieces of wood broken from limbs, or cut from a grapevine, that can be used over a hot fire for a quick smoke. They are not ideal for long smoking.

SAWDUST can be used to advantage for a quick burst of smoke. It also works nicely on some electrically heated smokers. An inch or two of moist sawdust in a pan, heated to the right temperature, will smolder for hours, producing lots of dense smoke.

LOGS AND WHEELS. Those people who cut their own wood for smoking purposes ought to consider logs cut short and split like stovewood. Wheels cut from limbs or small trees can be used instead of chunks. Also, logs can be used in large grills to bank the charcoal.

To be sure, I enjoy using various kinds of chips and chunks and logs, but, frankly, I prefer a few pieces of freshly cut wood to any of the packaged products. To me, freshly cut wood is not only better and cheaper but is also quicker. Thousands of backyard patio chefs across the land wait long hours every night for their chips or chunks to soak in water—when they've got a better green wood growing nearby, often just above their head, within easy reach of a bow saw or snippers.

My neighbor, on the other hand, insists that small limbs and twigs won't do. He prefers to fell green limbs about as big around as your arm and then cut them into wheels with a small chain saw. When the chain saw won't crank, he'll get out his foolproof bow saw to do the job.

After I thought I had completed this short text on smoke, I received in the mail a catalog of fancy foods and victuals from San Antonio, Texas. In addition to hot stuff, this publication listed a good many smoked meats for sale, at high prices, and I got to reading the text to see what they used for fuel and flavor. Page 13: turkey, hickory smoked. More turkey, hickory smoked. Page 14: ham, spiral sliced, hickory smoked. Page 15: duck, hickory; trout, maple; pheasant and quail, corncob; jerky, hickory; two kinds of smoked brisket, both hickory. Page 17: slab bacon and pepper bacon—both hickory. I checked through the catalog several times, and nowhere was even a mention of mesquite. What do make you of that, Watson? Are the Texans exporting all of the mesquite to Baltimore and Juneau?

COLD SMOKING

I have seen a number of schemes published in magazine articles for making smokers out of old refrigerators and barrels and wooden boxes. All of these may work satisfactorily, but this brings up the topic of curing meat by cold smoking at a temperature of below 100 degrees. Obviously, this meat is not cooked. Between the black and white of cold smoking and cooking, there is a vast gray area that scares me. Before you start building home smokers, you should decide whether you are going to cure meat or cook meat.

Usually, it is difficult to maintain enough heat for making smoke and at the same time hold the temperature of the smokehouse below 100 degrees. The problem is worse in warm areas such as Florida, and this is why "hog-killing time" is in cool weather. By far the best design for a smokehouse is a large walk-in unit with a small fire at ground level and racks of meat hanging above your head. To cure meat by this cold smoking method takes a long time. The larger the piece of meat, the longer the curing time. In the smokehouse on the farm where I was raised, my father smoked link sausages for 1 week, hams for 3 weeks or better. That's a long time to keep a fire going, and, frankly, isn't worth the effort unless you've got several hundred pounds of meat to cure.

In recent years the portable silo smokers with a water pan have greatly simplified the process of smoking while at the same time slowly cooking the meat. Since these units are available at a very reasonable price, they have, almost, become synonymous with smoking. Further, some small electric smokers with a removeable front, shaped like a small refrigerator, will also do a good job if the manufacturer's instructions are followed to the letter. And some of the accomplished patio chefs have learned to do a very good job of simultaneous smoking and cooking on a large covered-wagon grill.

There are some portable home "smokers" on the market which, it seems to me, sort of split the difference between cold smokers and cookers. These will no doubt do a pretty good job, but they can also get you into trouble. More than once, I have smoked chickens all day long—only to have to put them into my kitchen oven so that I could get them done enough to feed my guests before midnight. Plan on doing it that way, or take the trouble to rig your unit for cooking as well as smoking. In other words, cold smoke the meat at 100 degrees or below for several hours, then bring the temperature up to above 200 degrees for cooking. Sometimes an electric hot plate with a skillet full of wood chips in a suitably ventilated miniature smokehouse can be used in exactly this way.

The best bet is to build yourself a walk-in unit with good pressure-treated wood. Rig for burning green logs, or for smoking with wood chips or sawdust on an electrically heated coil with a heat-control rheostat. Such units are available today, along with fans and modern bug-proof vents, so that smoke curing meat is not as difficult as it was when I was raised on the farm. Perhaps this can be the subject of a future book, but the topic of this present work is smoking meat while cooking it, not smoking meat to cure it.

Remember that cold-smoked meat is usually treated in a brine or with a dry salt cure, and, in some cases, the recipes for a salt cure have carried over into modern hot smoking techniques. Usually, however, a salt cure is not necessary for smoking with most patio equipment. In fact, a lot of patio chefs these days are trying to reduce the salt in their diet instead of adding to it.

OPEN GRILL SMOKING

It's easy to get a little smoke flavor on your meat when you are grilling directly over hot coals. Simply put chips or chunks atop or around the hot coals. For a burst of smoke, very fine shavings can be added. Virtually all of the recipes given in Part Two can be smoke-flavored by this method. Of course, such smoke will be only a surface thing. A deeper smoke flavor can be obtained by using a closed hood for a longer period of time.

As a rule, beefsteaks are grilled quite close to the heat for a short period of time and therefore don't usually pick up much smoke flavor. This is usually all right because beef simply isn't much improved with a heavy smoke, in my opinion. Chicken is—and it is usually cooked for a much longer period of time, thereby being exposed to more smoke than beef.

COVERED GRILL SMOKING

For smoking, the advantage to having a hood on a grill is obvious. The importance of holding in the smoke is even more pronounced in windy weather, when the smoke from completely open rigs tends to blow away from the meat instead of rising up under it.

Kettle grills, and small covered grills of any sort, can be used for smoke flavoring, but the best job is done on the large covered-wagon grills where the fire is on one side and the meat is on the other. Pork roasts work exceptionally well with this kind of cooking and smoking, and pork tenderloin may well be at its best, provided that it isn't cooked long enough to dry out. Large chunks of meat also smoke nicely in the covered-wagon grills, partly because, being large, they have to cook for a long time.

Wood chunks are normally used in these units, and most people buy bags of these at the market and then soak them before cooking. It's much better to use larger green chunks or pieces of limb, and it's even better to bank the fire with a quartered green log. (Chips or chunks can be used in addition to the log.) Once the green log gets hot, it not only provides smoke but will also add to the heat. Toward the end of a long cooking period, green wood might well make the difference on whether more charcoal will have to be added. Another trick here is to bank the fire on two sides with such logs, then move them closer together as the charcoal burns down. A good deal will depend on how dry the wood is, how big it is, and so on. Remember also that a fire made entirely of wood works very well in these large grills, especially in those that have good draft control vents. Cooking entirely with wood is much cheaper than using charcoal, and the flavor of the meat is better. It really is. Further, a mixture of wood and charcoal is really a good way to go for meats that are to be cooked half a day or all day. Start with a charcoal fire as usual, then bank with wood. Add a little wood on top or on the sides for immediate smoke, then add more pieces as needed and as the charcoal burns out. Toward the end, you may have only wood. Adding wood in this way is better than adding briquets simply because it smells better and no doubt tastes better.

Those chefs who like the idea, but have no experience with wood, can easily proceed with charcoal briquets as usual, then work into wood as the cooking progresses. In any case, here are a few recipes to try on a larger covered-wagon grill:

Smoked Brisket

If you've got plenty of time, try cooking this recipe in your covered-wagon grill. The trick is to build a wood fire, or a charcoal fire, with plenty of wood chips, and then keep the fire burning as low as possible by closing down the vents.

> **beef brisket, about 10 pounds**
> **1 tablespoon salt**
> **1 tablespoon black pepper**
> **1 tablespoon paprika**

Build a fire on one end of your grill. Mix the salt, pepper, and paprika, then rub the mixture into the brisket. When the fire is ready, put the brisket onto the opposite end of the grill and close the hood. Cook for 12 hours or longer. The longer the better. You can turn it from time to time, but no baste is required. Exactly how long the meat should be cooked depends on the fire, the size and design of the grill, and the chunks of meat. The expert patio chef can tell when the meat is done by poking it with his finger or sometimes merely by looking at it. I prefer to use a meat thermometer.

Smoked Fresh Ham

Fresh ham is ideal for long, slow cooking combined with smoke. These days, I usually trim the skin and most of the fat off the outside of the ham before cooking it by this method. A whole ham can be used, or you can use either the shank end or the butt end. The bone can be left in. With either a whole ham or a half, it is highly desirable to use a meat thermometer to make sure that the pork is pretty well done—160 degrees.

I fresh ham	½ cup fresh lemon juice
I small can crushed pineapple	½ teaspoon cayenne pepper
I large onion, peeled and diced	4 or 5 cloves
I cup dry white wine	salt and pepper

Trim the ham and sprinkle it with salt. Rub some salt into the ends around the bone, then put the ham in a cool place until you are ready to cook. Puree the pineapple, onion, wine, cayenne pepper, and lemon juice in a blender or food processor. Build a fire in one end of a large covered grill. When the coals are ready, add some wood chunks to make smoke. Wipe the salt off the ham with a damp rag, then put it into a roasting pan of suitable size. Insert the meat thermometer, being sure to keep it well away from the bone. Baste the ham with the pineapple mixture and insert the cloves into the surface. Baste again, using all of the mixture, most of which will run down into the pan. Put the ham onto the end of the grill. Close the hood. Cook for an hour, then open the hood and quickly baste the ham with pan drippings and sprinkle it with salt and black pepper. Add more wood chunks if needed. Cook for another 2 hours, or until the internal temperature reaches 160 degrees. Baste with pan drippings from time to time, sprinkling lightly with salt and pepper. Add to the wood chunks as required. If you need more charcoal for the fire, it's best to light briquets in another container, burn them for 30 minutes, and then dump them into the grill—especially if you have the self starting kind. Pure charcoal can be added directly to the existing fire.

This same recipe can be used for other cuts of fresh pork, such as the Boston butt.

Smoked Fish

There are thousands of schemes and recipes for smoking fish, most of which require a special smokehouse. As discussed earlier, these are often rigged with an old refrigerator, a large drum, or some such container that can be fitted with racks or hooks. Often the heat is located well away from the box, and the smoke is conveyed to the meat with the aid of a flue of some sort. It's difficult to cold-smoke fish without such equipment. But a large covered-wagon grill can be used to hot-smoke and cook fish successfully. (Exact measurements aren't critical, but for best results the grill should be about a yard long.) Some accomplished backyard chefs make such a grill by cutting a 55 gallon drum in half lengthwise and fitting it with racks and hinges. In any case, the trick is to build a charcoal fire in one end of a long grill, add chunks of hardwood for smoke, and put the fish in the other end. The temperature should be maintained at 150 to 175 degrees and most fish should be smoked from 6 to 12 hours or so, depending on the size of the fish.

My favorite way to smoke by this method is to proceed with two or three fish of 3 or 4 pounds each. I leave the scales and skin on, but I cut both fillets free of the backbone, leaving the ribs intact. Then I soak the fish in a brine solution made with:

1 gallon of water
1 cup salt
1 tablespoon soy sauce
1 teaspoon Tabasco sauce

Mix all the ingredients. Put the fish fillets (skin side down) into a nonmetallic container and pour the brine solution over them. It's best to completely cover the fillets. Put the container in a cool place for several hours.

When you are ready to cook, put the fish on a rack to drain. Place the fillets scale-side down. Build a *small* charcoal fire in one end of the grill, getting it as close as possible to the end and as far as possible from the fish. I use two bricks butted together to help contain the coals. Add some seasoned hardwood chunks that have been soaked in water—or use chunks from freshly cut green wood, which I prefer for smoking. Put your fish

151

(scale-side down) on the end opposite the fire, with the tails at the very end of the grid. In other words, put the thickest part of the fillet the closest to the fire. Close the hood. Then prepare a basting sauce as follows:

1 cup peanut oil
½ cup onion juice
cayenne pepper to taste

Remember that a pinch of cayenne pepper goes a long way. Onion juice is available in bottles, but it's best, by far, to squeeze fresh onions in a garlic press. (Peel the onion and cut it into chunks to fit into the garlic press.) Mix the sauce and baste the fish with it every 30 minutes or so. The fillets don't need turning, and don't require constant attention. You may, however, have to add more charcoal and wood chips from time to time. It's best to use a hooded grill with a temperature indicator and an adjustable vent. Then you can adjust heat to about 160 degrees.

Smoke for 6 to 12 hours, depending on the thickness of your fish and the temperature. (If you can't keep the temperature down while at the same time maintaining a fire, reduce the cooking time.)

Although the above was obviously written for a large grill, the same ingredients and technique can be used in the smoker/cooker silo-shaped units, which have a heat source and wood chips in the bottom, a drip pan with water just above the heat, and a rack or two up top. These units do a very good job and are very easy to use. My next door neighbor, Dan Webster, has a silo smoker/cooker heated by an electrical element. The temperature stays at 160 degrees, more or less, depending on the qualities of the day, and constant supervision isn't required. As long as a little smoke comes out the top, all is well and good.

Smoked Duck

Large domestic ducks are usually quite fat and require no basting during the cooking process. In fact, I always try to get rid of some of the fat. It's best to smoke duck at a temperature of about 210 to 220 degrees. At temperatures in this range, you'll cook the bird slowly enough for the smoke to do its work and fast enough to cause some of the fat to drip away. It is, of course, best to use indirect heat, or, at least, to have a drip pan under the bird.

**duck
red wine vinegar
seasoning salts**

Wash the bird and prick holes into the skin on the breast with a fork, but do not penetrate the meat. These holes will allow the fat to ooze out. Trim the excess fat from the rear of the body cavity and discard it. Rub the bird generously with red wine vinegar and sprinkle it inside and out with seasoning salt. (There are several seasoning salts on the market, but I sometimes make my own by mixing half onion salt and half celery salt.) Truss the wings and legs.

Build a fire. When the coals are ready, add some wood chips and adjust the vents until you get a temperature close to the range listed above. Place the birds onto the grid and close the hood. Smoke for 6 or 7 hours, or even longer, depending on the temperature and the size of the birds. Check the fire and the wood chips from time to time. When the bird is done, the leg will turn easily in its socket.

Domestic geese can be cooked by the recipe above, but they will require a longer cooking time.

Some wild ducks, such as teal, are quite small and won't require as much time to cook. Most wild ducks don't have much fat, and they may require constant basting or perhaps barding with strips of bacon. This is especially true of fish-eating ducks that have been skinned, as well they should be. Ducks that have been feeding on fish instead of grain may require a marinade before smoking.

A silo-type smoker will also do a good job with this recipe, and a large kettle-type grill will also work, with proper adjustments to cooking time. Also see the recipe under "silo smoking" later in this chapter.

Hot Smoked Oysters on the Half Shell

Here's a recipe that works best in a large grill with a hinged cover. A small grill will do, but it will hold only a few oysters. Unless you are faster than I am, it's best to shuck your oysters and keep them on the half shell until you get enough to cook. Then, you can quickly transfer them to the grid and close the hood when you are ready to cook.

> **several dozen oysters**
> **I pound butter**
> **juice of two lemons**
> **I clove garlic, finely minced**
> **½ teaspoon cayenne pepper**

Build a hot fire in the grill and add some green hickory or hardwood chips that have been soaked in water. You'll need lots of smoke. In a saucepan, mix the butter, lemon juice, minced garlic, and cayenne pepper. Simmer for a few minutes, and let the mixture steep for a while.

Shuck the oysters, retaining some juice, and put them on the half shell on a table or on trays. Add about half a teaspoon of the sauce to each oyster. When the grill is ready and smoking, distribute the oysters on the half shell onto the grids and close the hood. Cook and smoke for 10 minutes.

Have saltines and toothpicks at hand and eat the oysters directly from the grill, provided that you eat them right away. (Leaving them on the grid or over the heat will overcook them.) If for some reason you want to serve the oysters on trays, use a heavy-duty rubber glove to handle them. Serve while hot. Enjoy.

Greg Rane's Tenderloin of Pork

For a sort of rambling dinner party, Greg Rane cooked up no less than 8 pork tenderloins. When I saw them, he had them stacked up like stovewood on a cutting board in the kitchen, where he was slicing one into wheels with an electric knife. "It's better," he said, "to cook more than you need, as they keep well in the refrigerator. I like 'em for lunch." He stuck a freshly cut piece with a toothpick and handed it to me for sampling, saying, "Once you feast on these, A. D., you may never again be satisfied with ordinary pork chops." Well, I hadn't been fed all day and didn't want to fool with toothpicks. For a while there I ate the pieces of tenderloin almost as fast as Rane could cut them. "The whiskey," he said, "is at the bar in the den. Kathleen will have the food ready to serve in a few minutes."

"Tennessee whiskey?" I asked, reaching for another piece of tenderloin.

Seeing Rane tighten his grip on the electric knife, I took the hint and slowed down on the tenderloin. But after the main meal, I wasn't the only guest who wanted seconds, and, in short, Rane had no tenderloin left for the morrow's lunch.

Later on, I wrestled the recipe from him, although he wouldn't be pinned down as to exact measures. He maintains, however, that it can't be cooked on anything except a large CB940 covered grill that is well seasoned.

"First," he said, "build a medium-sized bed of charcoal on one side of the grill. Start the fire and let the coals burn down for 30 to 45 minutes, until they are covered with a gray ash. When the coals are ready, lay the tenderloins on the opposite side of the grill. Baste the meat with a mixture of lemon juice, vinegar, melted butter, garlic powder, salt, and lots of good black pepper. Be sure to use garlic powder, as garlic salt won't do. It's best to melt the butter in a little pot and get it right hot, then mix in the other ingredients. After basting, sprinkle the tenderloin logs with a generous amount of lemon-pepper seasoning.

"Back up a little," he said. "Long before you start your fire, soak 10 or 12 hickory wood chips in hot water so that they will be ready. After you baste the meat and sprinkle each piece with lemon-pepper, throw 4 or 5 hickory chunks on the hot coals. Close the cover. You've now got 20 minutes to get a beer and make sure that your wife has everything under control in the kitchen.

"After 20 minutes, lift the cover, baste the meat, and sprinkle it again with lemon-pepper. Add more hickory chunks if needed. Close the cover. After another 20 minutes, spread the coals out and move the tenderloins directly over the coals. Grill for 3 or 4 minutes, then turn and grill the other side for 3 or 4 minutes. This sears and browns the meat, helping to make a more attractive dish. Cut off an end and eat it. Although most people think that pork has got to be cooked well done, tenderloin is better if it is served a little on the rare side. It's a lean meat, you see. When it's ready, take the meat to the chopping block and stack the pieces up like stovewood. With a good sharp machete—"

"You used an electric knife—"

"With your machete," he went on, not batting an eye, "chop each piece into wheels about ½- to ¾-inch thick. Put the pieces into a pan and pour the remaining basting sauce over it. Toss and tumble to coat all pieces. Then stand by the meat with your machete in case some son-of-a-bitch tries to eat all of it before your wife gets the other stuff ready to serve."

As explained in the first part of this section, the large covered-wagon grills work best for this kind of cooking and smoking. If you don't have such a grill, you can get by with a smaller covered-wagon unit, or with a kettle grill. On an open grill, you may be able to rig some sort of cover over the meat to help hold in the smoke. A tent of aluminum foil, for example. Or a large roasting pan, inverted. In short, not having a large grill should not prevent you from taking advantage of smoke in your cooking. Any covered grill can be used for indirect cooking (or a combination of direct and indirect) along with wood chips for smoking. In general, it's best to select meat that packs well in a small place, such as a Boston butt, instead of spreading out, like spare ribs. It also helps to choose a meat that lends itself well to smoking, such as pork or Spanish mackerel, as used in the recipe below.

Smoked Mackerel

Although it is none too good when fried, the Spanish mackerel is an excellent fish for the beginner to smoke or grill on the patio.

Dress the fish and season it inside and out with salt and pepper. Build a fire in a kettle grill or covered-wagon grill that has a hood, or use a silo unit. Because of the fish's oil content, it's hard to go wrong with any of these units, unless you undercook or overcook the fish. Testing the flesh with a fork is the best guide. Anyhow, build a good charcoal fire, add some chips, and you're in business.

Because of its oil content, however, it's best to watch for fires if you put the fish directly over hot coals. If you use a kettle grill, consider putting a water pan directly under the fish and arrange the coals and wood chunks around the pan.

STOVETOP SMOKING

In recent years, magazines and TV chefs have been touting a stainless steel box that can be used on top of the stove, or over hot coals, to smoke precooked meats. The rig has a tight-fitting lid, a handle, and a rack inside. The trick is to sprinkle some wood dust onto the bottom, put the precooked meat onto the rack, close the lid, and put the box over heat for a few minutes. It works pretty well, too. The units that I have seen advertised cost about $50 and come with a recipe book. Of course, variations of the design are sure to follow, so the best bet is to follow the manufacturer's directions.

Actually, the method is nothing new. The Chinese have been smoking meat in this manner for many years. Instead of wood, however, they often use tea leaves to make the smoke.

Before buying a stovetop smoker, as I call them, why not experiment with your Dutch oven or similar piece of cookware that has a tight fitting lid? Simply put a piece of aluminum foil on the bottom, sprinkle on some sawdust, put in a rack or stainless steel trivet, and place the rig on high heat until smoke comes pretty well. Immediately take the rig off the heat, put the meat on the trivet, cover tightly, and let it sit, without removing the cover, for 15 minutes.

Here are a couple of easy recipes to try:

Smoked Fish Fillets

If you are using the Dutch oven rig to smoke the fish, note that you can also use it to steam or poach the fish. For steaming, merely pour a little water into the Dutch oven, bring to a quick boil, arrange the fish on the rack or trivet, put into the pot over the water, cover tightly, and steam for a few minutes. Usually, 10 minutes per inch of thickness will be just right. After steaming, carefully remove the fish (still on the trivet) and dry out the pot. Salt and pepper the fish to taste, and brush both sides with a little olive oil or bacon drippings, and put it aside until you rig the Dutch oven for smoking, as directed above.

You can also poach the fish, and I often do this when I cook my own catch. Take a 2– or 3–pound walleye, smallmouth bass, or lake trout. Skin the fish, then fillet it. Place the head and bony parts into the Dutch oven and cover with water. Add salt and pepper and a large chopped onion. Bring to a rapid boil. Add the fillets and simmer for about 8 to 10 minutes, depending on the size of the fish. (The 10 minutes per inch of thickness will be about right, measuring the thickest part of the fillet.) Carefully drain the fillets on absorbent paper. Dry out the Dutch oven and rig for smoking, as described above.

Smoked Tongue

Boiled tongue, when sliced and served atop a cracker with a little brown mustard, can be one of the finer culinary pleasures afforded by the variety meats. Usually, the tongue is boiled for an hour or longer (until tender) in water and spices. For tongue that is to be smoked, I omit all the spices except for salt and red pepper flakes. After the tongue has boiled until tender, let it cool. Skin it, then cut it crossways into ½-inch slices.

Rig your stovetop smoker as described above. Lightly brush the sliced tongue with melted butter, then smoke it for a few minutes. Served hot or cold with crackers, it is hard to beat. Tongues of beef, lamb, and other animals can be smoked to advantage. In Finland, smoked tongues of reindeer are a delicacy—*savustettua poron kielta.*

Smoked Chicken Fingers or Livers

Cut the breast fillets lengthwise into fingers about an inch wide. Chop an onion. In a skillet, sauté or stir fry the chicken and onion in oil until tender, stirring in a little salt and pepper as you go. Transfer the chicken to the stovetop smoker, but retain the oil and onions. Smoke the chicken as directed above. Before serving, brush with some of the oil left in the skillet, or spoon a little of the oil and onion onto the chicken fingers before serving. You can also cook the whole breast fillets in this manner.

Try the exact same recipe for chicken livers. After smoking, put the livers back into the oil and sauté them for a few more minutes before serving.

SILO SMOKING

These units are quite easy to rig for smoking, and I am especially fond of the electric units for this purpose. Most of these have a pan to hold the wood chips, and this works very well. (Some manufacturers recommend that you use dry chips, and others recommend that you soak them in water prior to use.) A friend of mine who works at an electric utility company uses one that is marketed by his firm. He says that he throws out the pan and puts two green limbs, about the size of your arm, directly onto the heating elements. That way, he says, you get plenty of smoke and don't have to add chips frequently. The charcoal units also work nicely, but they can be a pain in the neck when the fire burns out and you have to replenish the coals. With some models, you'll need gloves to remove the meat racks and the water pan.

When using either the electric unit or the charcoal unit, remember that water must be kept in the pan if these units are going to cook slowly. When used without water, most of these units quickly become hot, like kitchen ovens, and will dry out your meat.

Smoked Leg of Lamb

Onions, parsley, and the other ingredients in this recipe go nicely with lamb, and this recipe for slow cooking and smoking works wonders.

1 7 to 9 pound leg of lamb	**1 teaspoon rosemary,**
1 medium onion	**crushed**
3 cloves garlic	**4 tablespoons butter,**
1 tablespoon chopped fresh	**melted**
parsley	**juice of 1 lemon**
	salt and pepper

Bone the leg of lamb and rub it inside and out with about half the lemon juice. Finely chop the onion, garlic, and parsley, then sauté them in melted butter for a few minutes. Stir in the remaining lemon juice and rosemary. Open up the boned lamb. Salt and pepper the inside lightly, then spread the onion mixture on the surface evenly. Tuck in the shin meat (small end) and roll the lamb. Tie with twine. Salt and pepper the outside lightly.

Build a fire in your silo cooker, or turn it on if it is electrically heated. Add wood chips. Fill the water pan. Put the meat in the center of the rack and smoke for 4 or 5 hours, or until done. The best bet is to insert a meat thermometer into the lamb and cook until it reaches 150 to 160 degrees for medium rare.

Easy Smoked Roast

I've always been fond of an easy-to-fix recipe for beef roast made in a crock-pot with a little wine and dry onion soup mix. The same ingredients can be used to advantage in a silo smoker. With a bonus: smoke flavor. Here's all you'll need:

> 1 5 or 6 pound boneless beef roast
> 1 cup good red wine
> 1 envelope onion soup mix
> salt and pepper

The night before the feast, put the envelope of soup mix on a flat surface and roll it with a rolling pin to help pulverize the contents. Mix a little salt and pepper into the mix, then roll the roast in it, coating all sizes. Put the roast and any remaining mix into a heavy plastic bag, then pour in the wine. Put into the refrigerator overnight, turning from time to time.

About six hours before you will be ready to eat, rig your silo unit for smoking. Put the roast in the center of the rack. Smoke for five hours, or until the meat is done to your liking. It's best to use a meat thermometer and cook until the temperature reads from 140 to 150 degrees (for medium rare). Leave the roast undisturbed, but quickly check every few hours to be sure that you've got water in the drip pan. It's easy to ruin a beef roast by cooking it too long, which can easily happen if your water runs out.

Larger cuts, such as a whole rump roast, can be cooked by the same method. Merely increase the cooking time. With electric units, this won't be a problem, provided that you keep water in the pan; with charcoal units, however, you may have to add more fuel.

Silo Duck

Beyond a doubt, a domestic duck is one of the best things that you can cook and smoke on a silo unit. I always allow half a duck per person, but the meat is quite filling, so that a tighter measure can be allowed. Thus, two ducks will serve from 4 to 8 people. If in doubt, stuff the birds with a bread filling of your choice. I've heard people say that the stuffing is better than the duck—but not if you are as fond of the dark rich meat as I am!

2 5-pound domestic ducks
1 cup soy sauce
¼ cup honey
¼ cup dark brown sugar
2 teaspoons powdered
   mustard

2 cloves garlic, crushed
1 tablespoon grated fresh
   ginger root
salt and pepper
sherry (optional)

Trim the excess fat from the rear end of the ducks. Salt and pepper it inside and out, lightly. Mix the other ingredients. Put the birds into a large plastic bag and pour the mixture over them. Refrigerate for 5 or 6 hours, or longer, turning the bag over from time to time.

Rig the silo unit for smoking. Take the ducks out and sprinkle lightly with salt and pepper. Stick a fork into the breast skin several times to allow fat to seep out during cooking, but do not penetrate the meat. Pour any remaining marinade into the water pan, then fill it with hot water. Put the birds onto the rack, breast side up. Close the hood and cook for 5 or 6 hours, or until the duck legs move easily in the socket. About 20 minutes before taking the birds out of the silo cooker, brush the breasts lightly with sherry.

Smoked Mallards

Mallards and some other wild ducks can be smoked quite successfully, but most of these do not have nearly as much fat as a domestic duck and some of them have a strong flavor if they have been feeding heavily on fish. I recommend that the birds be skinned and wrapped in cured bacon before smoking. Here's what you'll need.

ducks
bacon
celery salt
black pepper

Draw and skin the birds very soon after bagging them, then age them in the refrigerator for several days. If you have reason to believe that the birds have a fishy flavor, marinate them overnight in a solution of 1 tablespoon of baking soda per quart of water, or in whole milk. When you are ready to cook, build a fire in one side of your grill and add some wood chips. When the coals have burned down, close down the vents so that you will have a low temperature.

Sprinkle each bird inside and out with celery salt and black pepper. Wrap the birds with bacon, which should be pinned down with toothpicks. Pull in the wings and wrap them along with the breast. Draw the legs together, tie, and wrap both of them. The entire duck should be covered with bacon, leaving no more than ¼ inch between the strips.

Build a fire in your silo smoker, or turn on the electric heat. Add chips and fill the water pan. Smoke the ducks, breast up, for about 4 hours. Be sure to keep plenty of water in the pan, lest the birds dry out. If you've got teal or other small ducks instead of mallards, reduce the cooking time considerably.

Smoked Fryers

It's quicker to smoke and handle chicken halves, or quarters, but there's always something special about having a whole bird on the table, especially when it is nicely browned. These days, chicken is so inexpensive (as compared to steak or duck) that I usually cook at least 3—more for a crowd. Leftovers can be used for sandwiches or smoked chicken salad.

> **2 or 3 fryers** (2½ pounds each)
> **1 cup good white wine**
> **¼ cup olive oil**
> **1½ teaspoons Italian seasoning mix**
> **1 teaspoon pepper**
> **salt**

Mix the wine, olive oil, pepper, and Italian seasoning mix (available in little spice jars or tins at your supermarket). Put the chickens into a large plastic bag and pour the marinade mixture over them, making sure that all surfaces, inside and out, are coated. Refrigerate overnight, or for several hours, turning from time to time.

Rig the silo unit for smoking. Space the birds evenly around the rack (or racks if you have four or more birds on a double unit). Cook and smoke for about 6 hours. The birds are done when the leg moves easily in the joint. If in doubt, cut into a bird at the thick part of the thigh. The birds should be very juicy around the bone, but not bloody. If you cook on double racks, remember that the birds on top may get done first.

Silo Turkey

A friend of mine has a 2-rack silo unit with electrical heat. With it he often cooks 2 turkey breasts—one for dinner and one for sandwiches. For smoke, he uses wheels of wood, but from a green hickory limb about as big around as your arm. Of course, he puts one turkey breast on the top rack and another in the middle, and he relies on the "buttons" that sometimes come with store-bought turkey instead of a meat thermometer. Usually, it takes all day to cook the birds, depending on the outside temperature and the wind, so that the water pan has to be refilled once or twice, and more wood has to be added to keep up a good head of smoke. The top bird gets done first. Seasonings? My friend uses salt. That's right. He sprinkles the breast on both sides lightly with salt and nothing else. No marinade. No expensive wine in the drip pan. Just turkey and smoke flavor and a little salt. Try it.

A whole turkey can also be cooked by this method. A wild turkey is hard to beat, and in my opinion is more juicy than a domestic bird. If you are using a charcoal grill instead of an electric unit, remember that you will probably have to add more fuel. Sometimes, it will take 12 hours or longer to smoke a large turkey. If you don't have a "button" and don't trust your luck, insert a good meat thermometer into the bird's thigh or breast, making sure that the end doesn't touch bone. Cook until the temperature reaches 180 degrees.

Most of us will want to put more than salt on a bird, and I am fond of coating mine with bacon drippings and sprinkling on a goodly amount of black pepper along with the salt. Add stuffing if you like. In any case, be sure to start with a bird that is completely thawed out. Frozen birds take forever to cook.

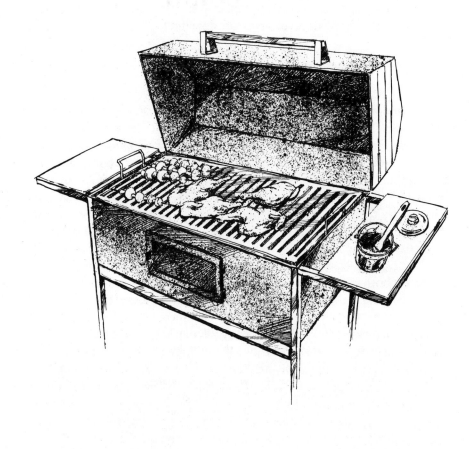

Part Five

BARBECUING

As an aid to cooking meat over an open fire or coals, the Arawak Indians of the Caribbean used a framework of woven green wood strips. The early Spanish explorers called the device *barbacoa,* from which came the modern American "barbecue."

Regardless of origin, the word has been used so loosely that it is now too broad to function definitively in a book like this. Even the term "pit barbecue" has different meanings and can be quite confusing. According to the directions set forth in many cookbooks, "barbecue" can be broiled or baked in the kitchen oven—or even cooked in a skillet. In short, the term means pretty much what one wants it to mean. Not too long ago, for example, I ordered what was billed as a "barbecue plate" in a small restaurant. What I got was a serving of very greasy, fresh pork with a little cold catsup dabbed on top of it. In the Deep South, where barbecue is something of a tradition, there ought to be a law against such advertising. Maybe there is in Texas.

Although I stand guilty of using the term loosely in the past, I say, for the record, that *real* barbecue is cooked over a wood or charcoal fire. Still, I won't disallow the good meats cooked over gas-heated lava rocks or electrically heated grills or silo cookers! And would I not be guilty of serious culinary sins by omitting, from a book like this, the Jamaican "jerk" or the Mexican *barbacoa?*

BARBECUE SAUCES—AND A RUB

A number of good barbecue sauces line our supermarket shelves these days, available in small jars and large jugs. And of course there are thousands of favorite personal recipes as well as the secrets of eating houses here and there across the land. Most of these sauces are quite thick and have a tomato base. This tomato sauce is, I think, part of what distinguishes barbecue from the grilled meats of Turkey or Mongolia or the South Pacific islands, since the tomato is an American gift to the world.

The trouble is that a thick sauce with a tomato base (or that contains sugar or syrup) is too often misused. It tends to burn, and doesn't work too well with meat that is basted every five minutes while being cooked for a long period of time or that is cooked quickly over very hot coals. This point is very important to a successful barbecue, lest the flavor of the meat be destroyed by the burnt taste of the thick sauce. If the meat requires basting in order to be succulent, remember that one can use a separate basting sauce, or maybe plain oil, and then use a barbecue sauce toward the end of the cooking period.

Some of the commercial barbecue sauces, as well as some personal favorites, have Liquid Smoke added to them. It's clearly a matter of choice, but I for one avoid the use of liquid smoke for those meats cooked over coals or flavored with smoke chips. But suit yourself. If you like to stand over your meat while it cooks, remember that a thinner sauce, often with vinegar and oil in it, is much better for long cooking and frequent basting, or mopping. As a rule, barbecue sauces made especially for beef tend to have some oil in them, and those made for pork have less oil. There are also regional favorites, and sometimes this will reflect the kind of meat that is preferred for the barbecue.

The recipes below contain both thick and thin sauces. Try all of them.

169

Bayou Bengal Barbecue Sauce

Here's a recipe that was, I understand, developed by the Animal Husbandry Department at Louisiana State University. The measures listed make up several gallons of sauce. Freeze leftovers in 1-pint containers for future use. You can also reduce the measures if you don't need a large batch.

I gallon catsup
½ gallon cooking oil
2 pounds butter
I gallon stock, made by
    boiling bones of beef or
    lamb (see below)
I bottle Louisiana hot
    sauce (3 ounces)
I large bottle
    Worcestershire sauce
    (10 ounces)

I jar prepared mustard
    (9 ounces)
4 pounds onions, chopped
2 cloves garlic, minced
2 pounds fresh or frozen
    okra, chopped
2 green peppers, finely
    chopped
4 large dill pickles, finely
    chopped

Boil the bones and retain a gallon of liquid. Add all the other ingredients and bring to a boil. Reduce heat, cover, and simmer for 30 minutes, or until the sauce is thick enough to suit you.

Variation: If you have a bumper crop of garden tomatoes, try peeling about 4 gallons and boiling them down until you have a gallon or so of thick sauce. Stir in a little vinegar and onion salt until it tastes like catsup, then simmer a little longer. Use the sauce instead of catsup in the above recipe. Some people may want to remove the seeds from the tomatoes, but I don't fool with them.

Walter Jordan's Hickory Pit Barbecue

Anyone who believes that truly good barbecue requires all manner of expensive sauces and exotic chips ought to consider Walter Jordan. An old black fellow in Maysville, Alabama, he built himself quite a reputation. Once, for example, he was commissioned to barbecue 8,000 pounds of meat for a governor's picnic! Although he cooked in a pit (or hole in the ground) covered by a grid, his method can be used in any large barbecue unit. Here's his recipe:

chicken, fresh pork, or beef (all in large pieces)
hickory wood
1 gallon vinegar
½ pound hot red peppers
juice of 3 lemons
salt

To make the sauce, put the vinegar in a large pan, then add the lemon juice and red peppers. Bring to boil, then remove the pan from the heat and let the mixture steep.

Build a fire of hickory wood in a large grill unit (or possibly in a pit). I prefer to use green wood, partly because it burns much slower and produces lots of smoke. It is, however, harder to start a fire with green wood. Of course, the more convenient wood chips and charcoal can also be used.

Salt the meat and put it on grids above the fire. The distance can be from 12 to 24 inches, depending on how hot the fire is. Ideally, the meat should cook for 6 hours without sauce. The fire should not be allowed to blaze up, and the meat should be turned from time to time. After cooking the meat for 6 hours, start basting it with the sauce. Turn and baste for another 4 to 6 hours.

Remember that thin ribs and small pieces of meat will not require as much cooking time. But also remember that the success of this recipe depends on slow cooking for a long period of time. It is not recommended for quick grilling.

For several years I lived in Huntsville, Alabama, and I frequented a small restaurant that served up chickens cooked by the Walter Jordan recipe. The chickens were always cut in half and cooked with the skin on. If you ordered half a chicken, that's what you got, along with potato salad and rolls. If you ordered a whole chicken, you got two halves, along with a bigger helping of potato salad and rolls. The restaurant had other items on the menu, but it seemed that most of the people came there for chicken.

If you don't have a pit barbecue and don't want to go to the trouble to make one, remember that the sauce recipe and cooking method above can be used on any large grill. Slow cooking is the key.

Bill's Hot Barbecue Sauce

A good many people concoct a barbecue sauce based primarily on a mixture of commercially available sauces. I've tried a number of these, and one of the best that I've come across—a rather hot sauce—came from a Tennessean by the name of Bill Arthur.

1 bottle **A-1 steak sauce** (26 ounces)	**juice and zest from 2 lemons**
1 jar **prepared mustard** (9 ounces)	**juice and zest from 2 limes**
1 bottle **Worcestershire sauce** (10 ounces)	**3 tablespoons chili powder**
	3 tablespoons black pepper
2 cups vegetable oil	**3 tablespoons red pepper flakes**
1 pound **butter or margarine**	**2 tablespoons Tabasco sauce**
4 cloves garlic, minced	**1 tablespoon salt**

Melt the butter in a saucepan, then stir in all the other ingredients. (It's best to scrape the zest from the lemon and lime peels, then discard the white part, along with the seeds and pulp.) Bring the mixture to a bubble, lower the heat, and simmer for 45 minutes. Use the sauce on beef, pork, or chicken. Leftovers can be bottled and kept in the refrigerator.

The first time you use this sauce, remember that it is hot. It's best to use it sparingly. I baste with it only after the meat is almost ready to take up, and I never use it as a marinade. If you want a sauce that is not as hot, cut back on the red pepper flakes as well as on the black pepper. Because I like the smell of black pepper, I'll often put some peppercorns into a piece of cloth and pound them with a hammer. Freshly cracked black pepper has a wonderful flavor and aroma.

Wes Gulley's Barbecue Mop

If you enjoy swabbing a sauce onto meat off and on for half a day, you need a sauce that won't burn easily. Avoid anything with sugar or tomato in it. Here's one of my favorites, which I adapted (or adopted) from *The Only Texas Cookbook:*

2⅔ cups beef stock
⅔ cup Worcestershire sauce
⅓ cup apple cider vinegar
⅓ cup peanut oil
1½ teaspoons powdered mustard
1½ teaspoons salt

1 teaspoon garlic powder
½ teaspoon ground bay leaf
1 teaspoon chile powder
1½ teaspoons paprika
1 teaspoon Louisiana hot sauce or Tabasco sauce

Mix all ingredients. This is a thin sauce and works best with a rag mop or store-bought dish mop. Use it every twenty minutes or so with meat that is cooked very slowly. Makes about a quart. I like it on chicken—or ribs.

Variations: If you don't have beef stock on hand, use chicken stock or turtle stock. Also, try 1 tablespoon of hot sauce if you like a hotter mop, as I do.

Chicken Sauce

This recipe will barbecue 3 or 4 chickens. These can be cooked whole by indirect cooking or they can be cut into halves and grilled directly. The recipe also works nicely with chickens that are cooked whole on a rotisserie. If you plan to cook on a gas grill that has an auxiliary eye for holding a pot, you might mix the sauce (except for the butter and minced onion) in the house and cook it in a small cast-iron skillet while you are waiting for the grill to heat up. In any case, it's best to apply the sauce thickly after the chicken has cooked for some time.

I cup red chili sauce
¼ cup butter
¼ cup dark brown sugar
¼ cup apple cider vinegar
juice of I medium orange
juice of 2 lemons
grated rind from I lemon
I medium onion, minced

4 cloves garlic, minced
I teaspoon salt
I teaspoon freshly ground
   black pepper
½ teaspoon dill seed
½ teaspoon celery seed

Melt the butter in a skillet or saucepan over medium heat and sauté the onion until tender. Stir in the other ingredients, reduce the heat, and simmer for at least 15 minutes, stirring from time to time.

Stonewall Jackson's Barbecued Rib Sauce

A jackleg genealogist in the family tells me that my mother was of Stonewall Jackson lineage, but, alas, really I can't claim that the recipe below was held secret over the years and handed down to me. Frankly, I got it from a work called *Bull Cook and Authentic Historical Recipes and Practices,* written by George and Berthe Herter of Minnesota. The recipe calls for a little Liquid Smoke, stuff that I've never been very fond of. But I'll allow that it does work well in this recipe, and I must point out that Herter declares Stonewall to be one of the first men to discover that the smoke flavor could be captured by way of tar deposits dissolved in water! In any case, the sauce, Herter says, must not be put on the ribs during the cooking. Rather, it is kept warm and spread on just before serving. Personally, however, I usually baste with it during the last few minutes of cooking.

I medium onion, diced (about 1 cup)
2 stalks of celery, diced (about 2 cups)
2 cups of tomato sauce (or 2 8-ounce cans)
½ cup water
juice of 2 lemons or limes
3 tablespoons butter or margarine
2 tablespoons dark brown sugar

2 tablespoons Liquid Smoke
2 tablespoons vinegar
2 teaspoons prepared mustard
I teaspoon salt
¼ teaspoon black pepper
¹⁄₁₆ teaspoon cayenne pepper (or 6 drops Tabasco sauce)
3 whole cloves, ground

Melt the butter in a cast-iron skillet. Sauté the chopped onion and celery. Then add the water and the rest of the ingredients. (Grind the cloves, or put them between wax paper and beat with a hammer.) Bring the mixture to heat, then simmer for 30 minutes. This sauce is especially good with pork ribs.

Note: The Herter version of Stonewall's recipe called for cooking the ribs slowly in an oven, then spreading the sauce over the ribs before serving. The ribs can also be cooked slowly in a covered grill, preferably by indirect heat. If wood or wood chips are used in the fire, omit the Liquid Smoke from the recipe.

175

Jamaican Jerk Rub

For most of us, the term "barbecue" denotes a juicy sauce of one sort or another that is swabbed onto the meat. But who could argue that the famous Jamaican dish called "jerk" isn't really a barbecue? It's made with a paste that is rubbed into the meat before cooking. Here's a basic recipe:

2 cups of chopped onion	**I teaspoon black pepper**
½ cup of chopped green onion tops	**½ teaspoon ground cinnamon**
hot peppers to taste (see below)	**½ teaspoon ground nutmeg**
I teaspoon ground allspice (Jamaican, if available)	**I tablespoon dark rum** (optional)
2 teaspoons salt	

Apart from the onion base, the key ingredients in all true jerk are allspice and hot peppers. (The allspice, a peppercorn-like berry, grows on a tree that is native to Jamaica; in fact, the purists will insist that jerk must be grilled on a fire made with wood of the allspice tree, called pimento.) How many peppers? And how hot? Suit yourself. Although the Jamaicans seem to prefer the Scotch Bonnet peppers, these are not widely available elsewhere. I suggest that you start with 3 or 4 relatively mild jalapeños, without seeds. (After removing the seeds of hot peppers, be sure to wash your hands before taking a leak. These things can burn you.) If you don't have hot peppers at hand, you can also use Tabasco sauce, your favorite brand of Louisiana hot sauce, or the Jamaican Pickapepper sauce. In any case, mix all the ingredients and mash it into a paste. A food processor will, of course, make a quick job of this. The paste can be put into a jar and stored in the refrigerator for a month or so.

This rub goes best with pork, the traditional Jamaican jerk meat. But it can also be used to advantage on beef, chicken, or lamb. With pork, it is rubbed into the meat directly, then the meat is covered and left outside the refrigerator for an hour or so before cooking. With lean beef or chicken, it's best to coat the meat with oil before adding the rub. I prefer bacon drippings for this purpose, but vegetable oil also works nicely.

Note: A dry jerk seasoning is also made in Jamaica, but it is usually used to sprinkle over cooked meat and other foods.

BARBECUE RECIPES AND TECHNIQUES

Many of the meats cooked by the recipes and techniques given in Parts One and Two can be basted with a suitable sauce and called barbecue. Nonetheless, I offer a few more recipes specifically for barbecue, along with a few techniques, such as pit cooking, that are not covered in any of the previous material.

Ribs 'n Beer Barbecue

Here's a dish that will melt in your mouth, as the saying goes. Before proceeding, however, make sure that you've got a suitable rig for steaming. I use a Dutch oven with a tight lid and a metal rack, or trivet, in the bottom. (Having some such rack in the bottom is highly desirable in that it keeps the meat out of the liquid.) I have also used one of those circular steamer inserts with a variable diameter, and I have found them to be satisfactory. If you can't find a suitable rack, build one with carrots. I have also used a wok (with lid) instead of a Dutch oven. Whatever the shape of your pot, it is important that you have a good lid that fits tightly.

The recipe will work with any sort of ribs, including those from deer and other big game. Just make sure that you've got enough meat to feed everybody.

ribs
beer
salt and pepper
barbecue sauce

Pour the beer into the bottom of your steamer and turn on the heat. (The measures aren't too critical, but I usually allow a can of beer for each 2 pounds of ribs.) Salt and pepper the ribs, then place them on the rack over the beer. Bring to a rapid boil, cover tightly with the lid, and steam for 30 minutes, or until tender. If you have tough Texas longhorn cows or old Florida brahmas instead of cornfed whitetails, the tenderizing may take an hour or even an hour and a half.

When the ribs have steamed almost enough, build a fire in your grill, warm up some barbecue sauce, and get out your basting brush or swab. When the coals are hot, place the ribs on the rack, about 4 inches above the coals. Baste with barbecue sauce. Cook 10 minutes on each side, basting several times as you go.

Any good barbecue sauce can be used with the ribs, and I much prefer one with a tomato base. I like a commercial mix called Cattleman's, which is available in small bottles or in gallon jugs. As a rule, any commercial mix is cheaper in large bottles.

My boys like the above recipe with lots of good bread and "beer" rice. Into the rice they mix some of the barbecue sauce. I like it too. Here's how I fix it: After the ribs have steamed in the beer, I retain the liquid and add enough water to make four cups. Add a little salt and bring to a boil. Add two cups of long grain rice and bring to another boil. Reduce heat, cover, and simmer for exactly 20 minutes. Don't peek. After 20 minutes, remove the pan from the heat and run cold water over the bottom of it. This will keep the rice from sticking to the pan.

Barbecued Pork Shoulder

Here's a good barbecue recipe for a whole fresh pork shoulder. I usually cook it with the bone in, but I trim off most of the skin. The fresh meat is best cooked for a long time in a large covered grill, using the indirect method described in Part Three, or in a silo cooker. Remember that fresh pork goes better than cured meat with barbecue sauce. Also remember that fresh pork must be well cooked to be safely eaten.

fresh pork shoulder	1 tablespoon prepared
salt and pepper	mustard
vinegar	1 teaspoon cinnamon
2 cups catsup	1 tablespoon soy sauce
juice from 2 lemons	black pepper to taste
1 clove garlic, minced	

Build a fire in one end of a large covered grill. Insert a meat thermometer into the end of the pork shoulder, being careful to avoid the bone. Wipe the pork shoulder with vinegar. When the fire has burned down to coals, put the pork shoulder into the opposite end of the grill and close the cover. Baste from time to time with vinegar, then sprinkle lightly with salt and a little pepper. Do not turn the meat. It will be done with the bone can be pulled out, or when the internal temperature reaches 170 degrees.

In a saucepan, put the catsup, lemon juice, minced garlic, mustard, cinnamon, soy sauce, and black pepper to taste. Heat and stir in a little vinegar until you get a consistency that you like in a barbecue sauce. Keep the sauce warm. When the meat is almost done, baste it with the sauce. To serve, slice the meat into chunks. Put the chunks into a bowl and toss with sauce.

Serve this pork with a good barbecue bread and hot baked beans.

Open Pit Barbecued Pig

If you want to hold a real barbecue, get yourself a 40-pound pig, some good hardwood, concrete blocks, and 6 pieces of iron rod. After scalding and scraping off the hair and gutting the pig, remove its feet. Saw or cut through the center backbone, but do not cut through the meat or skin. Then spread the pig open, butterfly fashion. The belly flab between the ribs and the hind legs should be trimmed away. It's best to butcher the pig several days ahead of time and let it hang. (Talk to your butcher.) Before cooking, bring the meat out of the cooler and rub it with vinegar.

With the concrete blocks, build a pit 24 inches high (3 blocks stacked atop each other), 4 feet wide, and about 5 feet long, blocking in the ends. Build a good hardwood fire in the pit. While the fire is burning down, put the pig atop a table and spread out the legs. (Have on hand two steel rods a little longer than your pit and 3 steel rods longer than the width of your pit. I use the ordinary steel rods made for reinforcing concrete. It's best to sharpen one end of each rod on a grinder. You can have the rods cut and sharpened at a local welding shop.

Now comes the tricky part. With the meats skin side up, run one of the longer rods into the shoulder about midway between the end and the center of the backbone; staying fairly close to the skin, run the rod on under the ribs, coming out where you cut away the flab. Now go in through the ham, again staying close to the skin. Run the other rod through the other side in exactly the same manner. Note that on either side the bulk of the hams and shoulders will hang low, and the ribs will be atop the rod. This method will permit the thickest part of the pig to be the closest to the heat. Next, pull the front feet forward a little and run a rod across the long poles so that it touches both front feet. With wire, lash the steel rods together where they cross, then lash the feet to the end of the cross rod. Put another cross rod in the rear. Run a third cross rod through the meat, about halfway where the flab was cut away, and also lash it to the long rods. Using both ends of the long rods, 2 people can pick up the pig, as though it were on a cot.

When your fire has burned down to coals, put the pig over the pit, leaving the long rods sticking out on both ends. The skin side should be up, leaving the exposed meat down. While the meat starts cooking, warm half

180

a gallon of water. Stir in a box of salt and half a small box of cayenne pepper. Turn the meat and swab it with the salt solution. Immediately, turn it again so that the exposed meat and body cavity are down.

Cook over coals for about 7 hours. You'll have to add more wood to the fire from time to time. It's best to burn the wood on either end of the pit, then rake the coals under the pig as needed. Or have a separate fire and put coals under the pig with a shovel. Remember to put more coals under the hams and shoulders. Turn and baste with the salt solution every 30 minutes or so, then turn immediately so that the skin side is not exposed to the fire for very long. (Also mop the skin side a few times during the day.) The times for basting need not be exact, provided that the surface of the meat is not allowed to burn or dry out. Remember also that the salt solution should be kept quite warm throughout the basting process. Cold water will cool off the meat too much.

The meat should be done in about 7 hours, more or less, depending on the size of the pig and the heat of the fire. When you figure that the meat is almost done, turn the pig over and baste immediately with a good barbecue sauce. The sauce should be warmed before using it. (A tomato-based sauce works best, and I recommend Stonewall Jackson's recipe, set forth above.) Leave the skin side down during this phase and cook the pig without turning until the skin browns and becomes quite crisp. Baste the other side several times while the skin side is browning. Note that the barbecue sauce is not put onto the skin side during cooking.

After the skin browns, take the pig to the table and start carving off the crisp skin. Put this into a pan, to be served separately from the meat. Then cut off chunks of meat and put them into another pan, adding some fresh barbecue sauce from time to time. For serving on a plate with potato salad, beans, or other food, chunks work nicely. If you want to use some of the meat for sandwiches, slice it off.

Note: Most any kind of hardwood can be used to build a fire of this kind. Dry or seasoned wood is easier to use, but freshly cut wood, once you get it hot, burns for a longer time and produces more smoke. Oak and hickory are especially popular. I recommend that you use "stove wood," split into pieces 2- or 3-inches thick and cut about 2½-feet long. The shorter pieces are easy to burn at the ends of the firebox, keeping a supply of coals ready.

Barbecued Chicken

Several of the chicken recipes in the other parts of this book could be called barbecue, and it is easy enough to grill chicken and then add some thick tomato-based sauce during the last few minutes of cooking. It is, however, a mistake to put a thick sauce on chicken at the outset and keep basting for a long period of time. In addition to burning, the sauce impedes the cooking and makes it difficult to tell when the chicken is done. A tomato sauce also makes it difficult to eat the chicken. In any case, here's a favorite recipe of mine, which requires a basting sauce for the cooking and a thick barbecue sauce for the eating.

5 fryers, dressed
½ pound margarine
juice of 5 or 6 lemons
½ cup vinegar
1 tablespoon salt (plus salt for sprinkling)
1 teaspoon pepper (plus pepper for sprinkling)
thick tomato-based barbecue sauce of your choice

Build a good fire in the grill. Cut the chickens in half and trim off any excess fat. (For the best results, use young barnyard chickens that haven't been fattened in a pen.) Squeeze a little lemon juice on the chicken halves, sprinkle with salt and pepper, and set aside. Heat the margarine in a saucepan, then add the rest of the lemon juice, vinegar, salt, and pepper. Heat to smoking, stir, and keep warm until you are ready to cook.

Arrange the rack about 8 inches over the coals and put the chicken on the grid. Turn and baste every 10 minutes or so until the chicken is done, which will usually take from 40 minutes to an hour, depending on the size of the birds, heat, etc. I also like to cook chicken for longer periods on a large covered-wagon grill, and by direct grilling over open campfire coals with the aid of my Big Foot rig, which will hold 8 chicken halves.

After the chicken is done, baste lightly with thick barbecue sauce and cook for a few more minutes. Note that the barbecue sauce is optional, so that you can serve the chicken either way or both ways. Allow half a chicken per person, or perhaps ¼ chicken for children and dainty eaters.

Note: For cooking a larger amount of chicken, see Dan's Auburn Club Chicken on page 122. After the chicken is done by Dan's method, you can add some thick tomato-based sauce and call it barbecue. For 50 chickens, you'll need about two gallons of thick sauce. Warm the sauce, then put it into a large pan or other suitable container. Dip each chicken half into the sauce and stack the halves into the cooker until you are ready to eat. Have plenty of napkins or paper towels.

Alaskan Ribs

Here's a recipe, one of my favorites, that originally called for big game ribs and a catsup made of highbush cranberries. The next time I head into the far north, I'll try these ingredients. Meanwhile, I can highly recommend the recipe for rack or pork ribs and cranberry catsup made from ordinary cranberries. Or mayhaws.

rack of ribs
bacon drippings
salt and pepper
homemade sauce (see below)

Build a good campfire and hang, or prop, a side of ribs beside it, close enough for slow cooking. Most people use green sticks to prop up the meat, but I cook mine with the aid of a Big Foot grill without the grid. I simply hang the ribs onto an S hook, and put the hook over the Big Foot arm. You can also rig an old dingle stick with a hook. If you use a side of pork ribs, as I do, remember to leave the sternum bone in place, which will help hold everything together.

When you are ready to cook rub both sides of the ribs with the bacon drippings, salt, and pepper. Then hang the ribs with the meaty side to the top. (If you have a hook on your mantle, remember that you can also cook a side of ribs in front of your kitchen fireplace, but remember to put a drip pan under the meat. The source of the recipe, *Alaska Magazine's Cabin Cookbook,* recommends that you rig a piece of heavy-duty aluminum foil on the rear side. But I seldom bother with this step.) When the ribs are almost

183

done, paint one side with barbecue sauce and heat for 5 minutes. Then paint the other side and cook for another 5 minutes.

The sauce can be made ahead of time, or during the first part of cooking, as follows:

I cup tomato catsup
½ cup highbush cranberry
 catsup (see below)
¼ cup oil
¼ cup vinegar
I large onion, finely
 chopped

I clove minced garlic or
 garlic powder
I tablespoon
 Worcestershire sauce
2 tablespoons chili powder
celery salt to taste

Sauté the onion and garlic in oil in a cast-iron skillet, then stir in the other ingredients. Simmer and keep warm until the meat is ready.

The highbush cranberry used in this recipe isn't a true cranberry, but it is similar. The "catsup" made with the berry is quite good, and can be used as a sauce for grilled lamb. I make it with regular cranberries (which can be frozen in season and used throughout the year). Here's what you'll need:

4 pounds highbush
 cranberries or 2 pounds
 regular cranberries
I pound chopped onions
2 cups water
2 cups vinegar
2 cups sugar

2 cups dark brown sugar
I tablespoon cloves
I tablespoon cinnamon
I tablespoon ground
 allspice
I teaspoon salt
I teaspoon black pepper

Heat 2 cups of water, cranberries, and chopped onions in a saucepan. Bring to a boil and cook until soft. Run this mixture though a sieve (especially if you are using highbush cranberries, which have lots of seeds) and return to the saucepan. Add the other ingredients, bring to a boil, reduce heat, and simmer until the mixture is thick. Put the catsup into sterilized jars and seal until ready to use.

In addition to using the catsup in the barbecue sauce, also try it as a sauce for lamb, pork chops, and other grilled meats.

A. D.'s Chunk Barbecue and Sauce

I like chunks of barbecued meat that are well-browned, almost crisp on one side and rather rare on the other. To accomplish this, I sometimes cook large pieces of pork directly over the heat. A grill can be used, but I prefer a campfire and a rack about 10 inches, or more, over a fire and coals made from green hardwood. The last time I cooked this recipe, I barbecued a fresh ham of pork over pecan wood. I used a Big Foot grill, but other rigs can also be used. The cooking time will depend on how hot your fire is, how big the piece of meat is, and the distance from the heat to the meat. For a 40-pound ham, start in the morning and cook until you have finished. Turning a large piece of meat can be a problem. With my Big Foot, I can swing the meat away from the fire and then turn it with the aid of thick gloves. If you don't have a Big Foot, give some thought, before cooking, to how you will turn the meat. Be careful.

After your fire has burned down somewhat, trim the skin and fat from the meat. Brush it with vinegar and sprinkle on a little salt and pepper. Cook on one side until the surface is browned and crispy, and the meat is done for about an inch and a half deep. Turn the piece of meat and start cooking the other side. Next, trim off the cooked portion of the meat, cutting it into chunks of an inch or two. Put the chunks into a crockpot or a slow-cooking cast-iron Dutch oven. Pour some barbecue sauce over the meat and stir it around, coating all the pieces. (For a whole ham, you'll need 2 or 3 such pots before you finish. It's best to fill up one pot before you start another. Before you finish a very large piece of meat, you may want to turn off the heat to one crockpot, lest the meat cook too much and fall apart.

The meat cooked by this method, and served directly from the crockpot, is ideal for making barbecue plates at a cookout or for fund-raising events. It is also very good for making barbecued sandwiches, in which case the meat should be cut into smaller slices.

Any good tomato-based barbecue sauce is good with this recipe, but I like to cook one with some fresh vegetables. Here's what I recommend for 20 or 30 pounds of boneless meat:

1 pound cured bacon, thinly sliced	**4 large onions, diced**
4 large tomatoes, peeled and diced	**2 cups red wine**
	1 cup Worcestershire sauce
12 cloves garlic, minced	**1 cup dark brown sugar**
4 cups catsup	**2 tablespoon salt**
2 cups vinegar	**2 teaspoons black pepper**

In a Dutch oven, fry the bacon and set aside. (Since only a few pieces of bacon will fit the Dutch oven, I usually fry some of them in a large skillet.) Pour off most of the bacon drippings and heat about ¼ of them in the Dutch oven. Sauté the onions and garlic for a few minutes, then add the chopped tomatoes. Add the catsup, vinegar, red wine, Worcestershire sauce, sugar, salt, and pepper. Also crumble the bacon and stir it in. Bring the sauce to a boil. Reduce heat, cover tightly, and simmer for 1 hour or longer.

This sauce should be used as soon as it is prepared. If you have only a small amount of meat, be sure to reduce the measures accordingly. Also remember that the sauce, containing bits of bacon and pieces of vegetables, works best with chunks of meat, as indicated above, and is not recommended for basting onto slabs of meat that are still being cooked. But be sure to try it with the chunks of meat cooked in a pit, as covered below.

PIT BARBECUE

Here's another barbecue term that is misunderstood, or is used in more than one way. Some jackleg commercial establishments advertise pit barbecue, meaning that it was cooked in a long grill, usually made with bricks or concrete blocks and fitted with a fire grate and a cooking grid or horizontal bars for holding the meat. To me, pit barbecue refers to meat that is cooked for a long period of time in a hole in the ground. Of course, a big fire has been burned in the hole (or over it), providing lots of hot coals.

If you tend to worry about things, it may be a mistake to put a hundred dollars worth of meat into the ground and leave it all night. Of course, most of us toss and turn while seeing burnt meat in the mind's eye. In truth, the opposite is more likely to happen, and you should be worrying about meat that didn't get done and soured in the ground. So, start with plenty of coals.

First, dig a large hole if you've got, say, a ham or two and a turkey. Or maybe a goat. Or mutton. The hole should be at least 4-feet deep, 4-feet long, and 3-feet wide. Build a fire in the bottom of the hole, then put tree limbs or long pieces of firewood across the top. As they burn in two, they will fall into the hole, contributing to the coals. Put more limbs across the top and continue until your pit is half full of coals.

While the fire is burning, salt and pepper your meat and wrap it with a clean cloth. Wet the cloth with vinegar. Next, wrap the meat in wet burlap. I use feed sacks that have been washed, and I like to get at least four thicknesses all around. Tie the burlap with heavy cotton string or hay bailing wire. Wrap around the middle part several times, until you get enough string with which to lift the meat and lower it into the pit. (Avoid nylon, which gives off chemical fumes when it hits the hot coals. Some wire will also give off fumes.) Using a strong pole with a hook on the end, lift the meat by the center string and lower it into the pit. Be careful. If you have more than one chunk, get it all ready before you put any of it into the pit. As soon as possible after the meat is put into the pit, scoop the dirt atop the meat and coals. Build a mound, using all the dirt that came out of the pit. Leave the meat all night and well into the day. Don't worry. It won't burn, although the bottom may be crisp. Dig out the dirt and remove the chunks of meat with the aid of a scoop. Carefully unwrap the burlap—but go carefully; the meat will be so tender and juicy that it might fall apart. Don't eat too much.

There are, of course, a number of variations on the above technique. Some people put stones into the bottom of the pit, and others put a piece of roofing tin across the meat, creating an oven-like hole under the ground. Some wrap the meat first in maguey, ti, or banana leaves, then follow with burlap. Suit yourself. Or use what you've got. Cabbage leaves will do. Or corn shucks. Maybe seaweed. Burlap can usually be obtained at your local feed store.

Other variations include sauce with which to souse the meat and covering. Most any thick barbecue sauce will work. The thick tomato-based sauces don't burn like they do when exposed to the heat, and really give a good flavor to the meat. I also like fresh pork treated with mustard. Some supermarkets or other food outlets sell prepared mustard by the gallon, and it's not expensive. Some old-time recipes call for treating the meat with ½ inch or so of lard (along with salt and pepper and maybe a little chili powder) before wrapping with the burlap or leaves. Lard is especially good on goat or venison, but it really isn't needed for pork or beef. Venison hams can also be wrapped with bacon to advantage.

A final word of advice. Have plenty of wood. Usually, it's best to have long some long pieces that reach all the way across the hole, as discussed above. Seasoned wood will work, but green wood can be used and makes very hot long-lasting coals. Of course, a good hardwood such as oak or hickory or pecan should be used.

Remember also that the above technique works best with large chunks of meat. To start with, try chunks of beef of about 15 pounds. Then try a large fresh pork ham.

Turkish Lamb

In Turkey and other parts of the Middle East, lamb is the main meat and has been for a long, long time. Cooking a whole lamb is often a festive occasion in celebration of a wedding, a newborn, or a holy day. Sometimes the head of the lamb is pointed toward Mecca during the cooking process. Actually, the practice goes back into history much further than Muslim or Christian religions, and may have come directly from the ancient custom of the sacrifice of the first-born child.

In any case, a very old recipe, called *tandir kabob,* is still used from time to time. In short, lamb is cooked in a pit without much ado. The bottom of the pit is lined with hot coals. The lamb is cleaned and gutted, then put directly onto the coals and covered up with dirt. After 6 hours or so, the lamb is taken out and the dirt and charcoal dust are brushed off. The bones are taken out, then the meat is sprinkled with salt, black pepper, and thyme. Potatoes and chestnuts are sometimes cooked with the dish.

In a similar recipe, *kuzo cevirme,* the lamb is put onto a pole and cooked over a pit of hot coals. After gutting and skinning the lamb, the meat is rinsed off and rubbed with salt, black pepper, and onion juice. The head is left on. The legs are trussed and the pole is placed across the pit over the hot coals. The lamb is cooked for 4 or 5 hours, turning from time to time. Basting the meat with a mixture of oil and onion juice is recommended.

Note: In the Caucasus, the Armenians and Georgians cook lamb directly on the coals in a pit and also on a spit, quite similar to the two Turkish techniques above. When cooked on a spit, the lamb is seasoned with salt and then basted with *kyurdyuk,* a special fat taken from under the tails of a certain kind of "fat tail" sheep that is bred in the area. This fat is often melted and used like butter in cooking.

Barbecue Bread

Cold rolls taken directly from the baker's box are often served with barbecue plates at large gatherings simply because it's the easy thing to do. If you are more interested in good food than in convenience, take the trouble to make some barbecue bread in your kitchen oven or on your grill, if you have enough room beside the meat. Here's an easy recipe: buy a long loaf of French or Italian bread and make diagonal cuts across the top. Brush it well with melted butter and sprinkle with garlic salt. Then sprinkle with grated Parmesan cheese. Wrap the loaf in aluminum foil and fold to seal. Grill for 20 minutes over coals, or until the bread is hot. This will take longer by the indirect method in a large grill.

Beans for the Barbecue

In some quarters, beans are traditionally served with barbecued meat. There are thousands of suitable recipes, many of which require long hours of preparation. By all means, cook a pot of Boston Baked Beans if you have the time. But if you're in a hurry, here's a recipe that is quick, easy, good, and different.

I can pork and beans
(16 ounces)
I can kidney beans
(16 ounces)
**I can speckled butter
beans** (16 ounces)
**¼ pound salt pork or
bacon**

I large onion, diced
½ cup catsup
⅓ cup dark molasses
I teaspoon dry mustard
I teaspoon salt
¼ teaspoon pepper

Preheat the oven to 350 degrees. Dice the salt pork and fry it in a large skillet. Remove the salt pork and add the diced onion to the pan drippings. Sauté for 5 minutes. Put the onion and pan drippings into a large bowl. Stir in the catsup, molasses, mustard, salt, and pepper. Open all the canned beans and drain. Dump all the beans into the bowl. Add the salt pork and stir until well mixed. Grease a combination baking and serving dish with margarine and dump the bean mixture into it. Bake for 30 minutes, or until the beans start a steady bubble. Serve on barbecue plates, along with the meat, bread, and salad or cole slaw. If you are feeding a crowd, use paper or plastic plates with 3 compartments. The beans can be served cold, but they are better when quite warm.

Other Go-Withs

Although baked beans are hard to beat with barbecue, a number of other vegetables can also be used. Potato salad and cole slaw are popular. Any good recipe for potato salad will be fine. The cole slaw, in my opinion, is much better when it is well drained and is served in a plate or tray with separate compartments. A simple green salad, with a little rice vinegar and a touch of olive oil, adds a refreshing touch to a heavy barbecue feed.

INDEX